Complexity Works!

Influencing Pattern-Based Change in Teams and Organizations

Denise Easton and Lawrence Solow

This book is dedicated to my family, whose unwavering patience and support for my crazy ideas has been an inspiration.

Lawrence Solow

This book is for my "A Team" – Harry, Claudina, Richard, Claudia and Lauren, who have unconditionally supported me as I have made complexity work in my life.

Denise Easton

Acknowledgments

We have been fortunate to have clients, colleagues and collaborators who have listened to our ideas, participated in early applications of the Complexity Space™ Framework and added their experiences and insights to our ongoing practice.

Thanks to our early readers, Lisa Kimball, Kathleen Lucas, Gregory Solow and Ryan Solow, whose comments on our initial draft of the book provided the "fresh eyes" perspective we needed to fine-tune our thinking and language.

On March 31, 2016, the day Larry and I completed the first draft of this book Zaha Hadid died. She was an architect whose visions of structures and space were groundbreaking and inspirational. Hadid described her firm's unique approach to realizing their boldest and challenging concepts as, "an organic language of architecture, based on new tools, which allow us to integrate highly complex forms into a fluid and seamless whole." This is precisely what the Complexity Space™ Framework strives to achieve – creating new ways to understand and influence complex, pattern-based change in teams and organizations.

Table of Contents

Preface

The Industrial Revolution provided many gifts that make our current way of life possible. In the quest for consistency and efficiency, "assembly line" processes and tools were created. Henry Ford's ability to mass-produce Model T automobiles revolutionized travel within the United States. Reinforced by the scientific management principles and tools of Frederick Taylor, identifying and utilizing the "one best way" to perform any task enabled suppliers to drive down cost and increase quality.

The search for more and more consistency and standardization led to statistical process control, Total Quality Management, Six Sigma, Lean Manufacturing, the Theory of Constraints and other improvement methodologies. Each of those concepts shares an assumption – that causes of inefficiency can be traced to root causes which once identified, can be eliminated and the system returned to its prior state of consistency and efficiency.

With over 100 years of practice, the advantages of this predictive, cause-and-effect mindset came to be taken for granted. No longer questioned, it became the assumed, natural, "correct" way to look at the world.

Providing a preview of the metaphor of viewing change through different lens or 3-D glasses (which we'll describe in greater detail later), this perspective became what we came to call the "Red Lens" Paradigm.

For all of the good things the Red Lens Paradigm offered, it did not consistently deliver on the premise that every issue can be deconstructed, decomposed, analyzed, prioritized, and fixed.

A second paradigm which we call the "Blue Lens" Paradigm (the other colored lens in 3-D glasses) has been recognized as a useful way to look at today's complex systems and organizations. Applying principles and distinctions from biology, complexity, chaos, catastrophe, and other non-linear sciences are critical for managing projects when the speed of change and number of variables increases.

Neither the Blue Lens nor the Red Lens alone offers the "one best, guaranteed way" to address all of the diversity existing in today's complex systems and organizations. We believe this new reality demands an adaptive, multidimensional and inclusive framework we've named the "Complexity Space™ Framework."

This framework embraces a "Both/And" approach to organization change and transformation by integrating both the Red Lens and Blue Lens Paradigms. Based on the situation, applying the appropriate amount of perspective from each lens offers the clearest view of options and actions for teams and organizations.

In the Complexity Space™, the following principles guide any action:

- Cause and effect may not be directly linked

- Levels of input/cause may not be proportional to output/effect

- There is no "one best way" to achieve desired results

- Systems are acutely sensitive to initial conditions

- Teams and organizations constantly evolve and self-organize

- Complex systems are most effectively and efficiently characterized by their patterns

We believe organizational change agents often return to concepts and tools that are most familiar to their organizations – even if they are not especially effective or appropriate for specific circumstances or conditions.

We have distilled a new set of language, distinctions, tools and lenses to help navigate the Complexity Space™. Even though we recognize that "everything influences, and is influenced by everything else" in complex organizations, we believe that defining and sharing the elements of the Complexity Space™ Framework will make it easier to understand, talk about, and influence change.

We have written this book with the direct and indirect input of clients who have recognized the need to make complexity work in their organizations.

If you are:

- Concerned about the health and sustainability of your organization based on issues that are happening right now, or are expected to happen in the next 3-5 years

- "Stuck" in your efforts to make improvement and sustainable change happen

- Concerned that status quo, "more of the same" tools won't address your team's or organization's needs

- Actively seeking new concepts and tools that are compatible with what you already know and use

- Looking for solutions that are robust and useful in a variety of situations

- Open, creative, nimble, and willing to experiment, recognizing that not every experiment will be successful

- Interested in people, teams, and systems

- Able to hold and appreciate the tension of conflicting ideas

- A formal leader or influencer who leads informally

Then *Complexity Works! Influencing Pattern-Based Change in Teams and Organizations* is for you!

Introduction

Every organization is confronting the consequences of an increasingly complex world. A major difference in the teams and organizations that appear to thrive is their ability to make complexity work for them.

This book explores the interplay between traditional, familiar options for achieving and sustaining business goals and new, unfamiliar ones. We'll look through the lenses, language, and distinctions of two different and complementary paradigms – Red Lens and Blue Lens.

We know the challenge begins when the goal is to get things done while everything is constantly changing. We believe that understanding, developing and improving patterns is how organizations grow, improve, innovate, and succeed — and having an (expanded) set of options for assessing, adapting, and aligning all the moving parts of the organization during constant change is better than a single solution. *If you give a person a fish, they eat for a day. If you teach them to fish, they can eat for a lifetime.*

Complexity Works! makes sense and works in large part because we take the stance that the Red Lens Paradigm of "one size fits all" solutions just isn't enough — it never was and never will be. As we guide you, the reader, through this book we will build the case for including our new Complexity Space™ Framework of organizational change to complement and expand those you already use.

The story we will share begins with the recognition that all businesses operate in a world where complex human organizational systems dominate. A new business model we call the "Complexity Space™ Framework" needs to take its place next to the established theories and practices of business management. Leaders need to move from (trying to and believing they can) control the system to seeing, adapting to, influencing and integrating the patterns of knowledge, people, systems, and networks out of their direct control.

Specifically, we hope to accomplish the following four objectives:

- Demonstrate how and why *Complexity Works!* through identifying and influencing the critical patterns of teams and organizations

- Provide theory, models and tools to create a new capability for adaptive change, grounded in intentional, precise and sustainable actions

- Accelerate "Pattern-based changeability" – doing things better, faster, cheaper

- Help build a culture of adaptive leadership, aligning the organization and engaged stakeholders

We hope the Complexity Space™ Framework offers fresh insights into the complex and interconnected relationships between your organization and the networks which are connected to it. We will have been successful if you can help your organization create a new "habit" of embracing rapid cycles of opportunities and disruptions by understanding and leveraging "Pattern-based changeability."

Part 1: Complexity Works! in Context

When we look back at the evolution of our work we were surprised to find that as early as 2009 we were already building the foundations of what would become the Complexity Space™ Framework. It is reassuring to know our initial gut instincts and persistent questions about what seemed true and useful have stood the test of time and continuing inquiry. What we can now confidently say is that the Complexity Space™ Framework is succinct and robust enough to add value to teams and organizations trying to create new possibilities for sustainable change.

In Part 1, we will set the context for understanding and working in the Complexity Space™. The book, like our work, has been a continuous inquiry into the most appropriate and adaptive approaches to describe the world in which complex human organizational systems operate. The metaphors for understanding this new paradigm are fundamentally different. As we help you discover the Complexity Space™ Framework, you will become familiar with new lenses, languages, and distinctions which will serve as guides during our journey:

- Seeing through a new lens to become aware of differences between what you thought was happening and what is actually happening

- Learning new language to become more precise in having shared conversations about those differences

- Using that language to highlight distinctions between the Red Lens and Blue Lens Paradigms that explain how each adds value to teams and organizations

We begin by presenting a simple but robust comparison of two divergent paradigms for managing and operating in organizations, the Red Lens and Blue Lens. In each, the point of view is similar in some areas and dramatically different in others.

We frequently share this story from the late writer David Foster Wallace's commencement speech to the 2005 graduating class at Kenyon College:

There are these two young fish swimming along and they happen to meet an older fish swimming the other way, who nods at them and says, "Morning, boys. How's the water?" And the two young fish swim on for a bit, and then eventually one of them looks over at the other and asks, "What the hell is water?"

Like us, our clients often knew that current practices did not offer an adequate way to recognize the water in which they were swimming, no less describe or discuss it. In Foster Wallace's conclusion we recognize a universal truth – that what seems simple and obvious is not always so:

"It is about the real value of a real education, which has almost nothing to do with knowledge, and everything to do with simple awareness; awareness of what is so real and essential, so hidden in plain sight all around us, all the time, that we have to keep reminding ourselves over and over: "This is water." "This is water."

We aren't fish, and when we do swim we generally aren't under water the entire time. When Denise shared this metaphor with a client he started to laugh and said he had an image of a CEO pounding a desk and saying, "Why can't we see what's happening? This is our business. This is our business."

In fairness to the CEO or any leader, it is incredibly difficult to see and be aware of the ocean of our teams' and organization's shared experience.

Next, we explore the concept of patterns. The twenty first century requires fundamentally different metaphors and language to address the most demanding and complex issues facing today's teams and organizations. As we assessed how organizations currently address the issues of productivity, resilience, innovation and disruption, it became evident that there is a struggle between traditional and new models, constructs, theories and practices, experiences and expectations. The role of patterns is critical to understanding and operating in the new paradigm.

In the final section of Part 1, we introduce the core elements of the Complexity Space™ Framework. Each of the elements provides a vehicle for more granular awareness and conversation about how to assess, prioritize, design, act on, and learn from attempts to make sustainable and adaptive change happen.

The good news: we have found these paradigms to be universal – they exist in every team or organization. Our concepts are also robust – they can be customized to each individual team's or organization's unique circumstances. Based on these new lenses, language, and distinctions, teams and organizations will gain new possibilities for changing their patterns of thought and action.

Paradigms

What is a Paradigm?

From dictionary.com:[1] [**par**-*uh*-dahym, -dim]

- a framework containing the basic assumptions, ways of thinking, and methodology that are commonly accepted by members of a scientific community.

- such a cognitive framework shared by members of any discipline or group.

- the company's business paradigm.

Larry tells this story to explain paradigms: "Paradigms are like wearing glasses or contact lenses. When you're wearing them, everything looks sharp and in focus. You don't pay much attention to the glasses, you just 'see.' It is only when you step back and take the glasses off that you realize you've been wearing them and that a different way of seeing things is possible. And by changing the prescription of your lenses, you literally change your focus."

---

[1] paradigm. Dictionary.com. Dictionary.com Unabridged. Random House, Inc. http://www.dictionary.com/browse/paradigm

"For example, if I put you in a pitch-black room and ask what you see, the answer is, 'Nothing! It's too dark.' But if I provide you with night vision goggles, all of a sudden you begin to see different things. The amount of light in the room did not change – your lenses did."

Notice that neither experience of seeing in the room is "good" or "bad." However, one may be more useful than another in dealing with particular situations or trying to achieve particular goals. If you are trying to go to sleep, not being distracted by infrared images is a useful thing! If you are trying to get to the other side of the black room, the night vision goggles provide a distinct advantage.

In this book, we will define two different, yet complementary, ways of seeing. Like the examples above, one is not better or worse than another – they simply focus attention on different things.

If we were to describe an organization as a machine, we would describe its design, (components) parts, and function and be fairly confident that what we described matches the actual machine both in appearance and intended output (use). Machines are valued for their reliability to operate pretty much as expected. In other words, the degrees of difference between what we expect and what we get are very small. Generally, machines are assembled from standardized components, which contribute to their cost effectiveness; and once the structural components are designed and tooled, the machine can be easily replicated.

On the other hand, consider the metaphor of an organization as a garden. Gardens are emergent and continually influenced by any number of factors (weather, soil quality, seeds, fertilizer, etc.). Although gardens are designed, can have parts and a designated "function" (flowers vs. vegetables), the garden is alive and the practice of growing and cultivating is continual.

We use these two metaphors because they offer a fundamental understanding of the differences that make a difference between a predictive/mechanistic/linear view (Red Lens) and an organic/complexity (Blue Lens) view of an organization. At all times, both inform how we make decisions and manage our organizations.

We begin with a brief exploration of the theory that underpins each paradigm. From there we'll explore the interdependence and linkages between them and their ability to expand the view of the "where, how, and why" of organizational productivity, advancement and transformation.

The Red Lens Paradigm

Long before the Industrial Revolution and the broad scale institutionalization of industrial management practices, people have sought to understand how humans work and live together. The Industrial Revolution which began in the mid-eighteenth century laid the foundation for a new paradigm of how to view the world to achieve advancements in the quality of life, the productivity of man, and the efficiency of organizations.

In the early 1900s, Frederick Taylor identified and developed his scientific principles of management. These focused on the interdependence of human and machine working together for maximized product value.

Opportunities for continual improvement and efficiency were firmly aligned with the experience of businesses which recognized high levels of certainty and predictability as the natural drivers for success. Once business leaders could implement the "one best way" to perform any task, they could more quickly drive down cost and drive up quality.

It is not a coincidence that the "assembly line" mentality and management theories, when combined with powerful new mechanisms from materials to manufacturing, revolutionized everything from travel to skyscrapers to the rise of the production worker (man viewed as a machine). But this was only a beginning of how the linear view of the world would solve the biggest problems confronting business and institutional success.

The search for more consistency and standardization led to statistical process control, Total Quality Management, Six Sigma, Lean Manufacturing, the Theory of Constraints and other improvement methodologies. Each of those concepts shares an assumption – that causes of inefficiency could be tracked back to root causes which, once identified, could be eliminated and the system returned to its prior state of consistency and efficiency.

With over 100 years of success, classical management theory developed a loyal following in large part due to the alignment of the machine metaphor and the practice of focusing on "one best way" to perform and manage tasks. This view became what we call the Red Lens Paradigm.

The Red Lens Paradigm is characterized by:

- Physicality (can be seen and touched)
- Ability to be assembled and disassembled (fixed)
- Operated relatively easily (controlled)
- Highly predictive nature

For all of the good things the Red Lens Paradigm offers, it may no longer be the most useful way to look at today's complex systems and organizations. The sheer number of details or moving parts frequently obscures cause and effect relationships, making purely "rational" decision-making ineffective. We recognize there are too many variables to believe every issue can be deconstructed, analyzed, prioritized, and the "one best, guaranteed way" implemented to address all of that complexity.

The Blue Lens Paradigm

Complexity science is a highly interdisciplinary approach that is rooted in mathematics, the physical, biological and social sciences, and most importantly on the inherent non-linear dynamics of certain kinds of systems. Complexity science also offers something that most management theories do not, a basis for understanding the fundamental characteristics, deep nature, structure and patterned behavior of organizations as systems.

The following three areas of complexity science play particularly important roles in setting the context for an organization to help explain and view itself as an emergent, nonlinear system:

Chaos Theory explains the behavior of complex systems whose behavior is sensitive to slight changes in conditions, so that even the smallest action or change can give rise to significant consequences. The "butterfly effect" is an example of how something as small as the flapping of a butterfly's wings can influence weather patterns.

Nonlinear Dynamical Systems offer new language and critical insight into phenomena such as attractors, bifurcations, chaos, fractals, catastrophes, and self-organization, all of which describe systems as they change over time.

Complex Adaptive Systems (CAS) consist of groupings (from teams to business units to an entire organization) of individual agents, who have the freedom to act and react in unpredictable ways, and whose actions are interconnected such that they produce system-wide patterns.

When businesses refer to complexity, it is often associated with the inner workings of an organization – its structural components. Within a complex organizational structure such as a team or organization, complexity refers to the manner in which the system behaves relative to its structure – the aggregate behavior of everyone with a relationship to the organization cannot be fully understood by simply seeing or responding to individual "parts."

The power of such Complex Adaptive Systems (CAS) is their ability to allow a massively entangled group of diverse individual "agents" the freedom to be adaptable and resilient. It is this dynamic that enables a CAS to undergo spontaneous self-organization, keeping the system healthy and adaptive. This is a very different metaphor than that of a machine.

The Blue Lens Paradigm is characterized by:

- Indirect linkages of cause and effect
- Levels of input/cause may not be proportional to output/effect
- No "one best way" to achieve desired results
- Acute sensitivity to initial conditions
- Continual emergence, evolution and self-organization
- Patterns of behavior, processes and structure

Complexity Science and Business

Complexity entered the mainstream media and the boardroom in 2010 when IBM's annual survey of 1500 CEOs focused on Capitalizing on Complexity. This one white paper did more to bring the issue of complexity front and center as a dominant business challenge than numerous highly regarded academic articles.

Complexity had become a business problem that required business-focused solutions. The CEOs' clear acknowledgment that, "a rapid escalation of complexity is the biggest challenge confronting them," and that, "their enterprises today are not equipped to cope effectively with this complexity in the global environment,"[2] sounded an alarm to those helping organizations understand and manage complex business environments.

Instead of exclusively relying on hierarchies, centralized control, cause and effect discipline, division of labor, standardized procedures, and emphasis on planning rather than improvisation, the Complexity Space™ Framework (CSF) provides an expanded vocabulary and new metaphors. The CSF integrates the adaptive and responsive qualities of seeing, adapting, influencing and changing patterns for incremental and continuous change throughout the organization.

In this section, we introduced two lenses for viewing organizations – the Red Lens and the Blue Lens. In comparison to the more structured, sequential Red Lens Paradigm, a complex and emergent view of organizations requires a significant change in how to conceptualize management strategies and leadership.

---

[2] IBM CEO survey, 2010, Capitalizing on Complexity

When viewing their teams and organizations through the Blue Lens Paradigm, business managers acknowledge that they are not really able to control everything that is happening in their spheres of influence. It is essential they become skillful and intuitive masters of adapting to a continuous state of change. It is not simply a matter of efficiently moving from one unanticipated scenario to the next. The real talent is to move through the current state to the anticipated desired state with greater agility and fewer surprises.

In the next section, we will focus more attention on one of the most critical differences between the Red Lens and Blue Lens Paradigms –Patterns.

Patterns

When we first encountered the theory and use of patterns in our work, we immediately recognized the need to define, simplify and integrate this concept into language and applications for business practices.

As we considered the distinctions and tensions between the Red Lens and Blue Lens Paradigms, the following questions were essential to our inquiry:

- What is the advantage of patterns versus predictions?

- How do we use patterns in our more traditional practices?

- How do patterns emerge in the diverse domains of organizations?

- How do we change patterns?

- Why are patterns the go-to place when you are stuck?

- How can we distinguish patterns happening at different levels, between different groups, throughout the system?

Working with patterns affords greater agility and insight into the relationships among the parts of the organization which are often unrecognized or invisible but still essential to the overall health and development of the business.
People continually generate activities throughout their teams, departments, functions, and organizations, leading to results which create both intended and unintended consequences that influence both the individual and collective systems' patterns of behavior.

We believe the development of lenses, language, and distinctions regarding patterns are critical to understanding the relationship between those individual human behaviors and Complex Adaptive Systems. Unlike the uncomfortable metaphor of humans as machines, the image of intricate and beautiful patterns better reflects the nuances of humans bound together in complex systems.

Properties of Patterns

Let's define what we mean by a pattern.

From Dictionary.com: [3]

- A pattern is a combination of qualities, acts, tendencies, etc., forming a consistent or characteristic arrangement.

---

[3] pattern. Dictionary.com. *Dictionary.com Unabridged.* Random House, Inc. http://www.dictionary.com/browse/pattern

You may be most familiar with the concept of patterns in nature. Why do the leopard's spots create a pattern?

Thinking about leopards and the patterns of their markings is an excellent example of how patterns and their creation are part of the genetic code of any complex system – biological or organizational.

Those patterns exist for good reasons. In the case of the leopard, they provide camouflage, allowing the animal to blend in with its surroundings to provide a competitive advantage when hunting.

Patterns in the organizational context are how we recognize, understand, discuss and work with the unique experiences (behaviors), structures and actions/reactions in teams and organizations over time and space. For these reasons, patterns are critical to developing an understanding of the Blue Lens Paradigm, and offer an important way to talk about and explain how human systems resemble and act like Complex Adaptive Systems.

The ability to recognize, understand and use patterns to influence what is happening throughout the organization is the number one distinction of working with the Complexity Space™ Framework.

When you can see and understand the properties of organizational patterns, you can more effectively focus on areas for action:

- Patterns in the Blue Lens Paradigm give shape to the context of action occurring in the specific complex active system (organization)

- Patterns are a unique combination of behaviors, acts, qualities or events that repeat themselves over time and space

- Patterns are both unintentional and intentional

- Patterns demonstrate unique configurations that are both substantial enough to be observed, studied, and analyzed, and robust enough to be manipulated and changed without destroying their value in sustaining the overall organization

- Patterns traverse traditional (linear) and complex (non-linear) methodologies, models, actions, etc.

The importance of establishing a practice or guide for pattern-centric continuous inquiry cannot be emphasized enough. Each time we ask the questions below about team or organizational patterns, we create an opportunity to discover a new piece of information, evaluate how our intentional and unintentional actions have influenced any particular pattern-based action and adjust what we do next.

- How do we see them?
- What do we do when we find them?
- How can we use them?
- How do we change them?

Introducing the Complexity Space™ Framework

The Complexity Space™ Framework is a scale-free framework for understanding and influencing organizational patterns. It not only recognizes but embraces both linear and complex influences and practices.

Complexity Space Framework

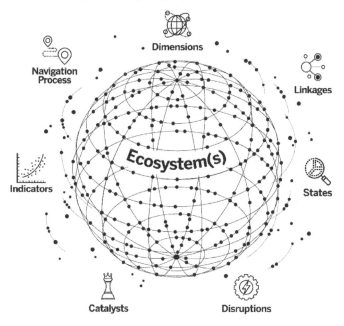

We first recognized the need to look beyond the dominant Red Lens Paradigm when we asked one simple question – How do organizations see, understand and influence the deeply entangled patterns within their complex environments?

When we began our conversations in 2009, we talked about how to introduce a new set of tools for making change happen that integrated the Red Lens and Blue Lens Paradigms. Over time, we came to believe the Complexity Space™ Framework is more than a model or practice that fits within either paradigm – it is a new and unique framework for sustainability and transformation.

The Complexity Space™ Framework is not "more of the same," nor is it a repackaging of the *same old stuff in a new container.* The CSF is a new construct for navigating an organization's complex patterns. This new framework contains its own language, distinctions, and tools.

The Complexity Space™ Framework at a "twenty-thousand-foot view" holds the patterns generated within, between, and across networks of internal and external Ecosystems (a critical distinction we'll define shortly) that are part of Complex Adaptive Systems.

As shown in the diagram on page 35, the Complexity Space™ Framework is comprised of eight core elements: Ecosystem(s), Dimensions, Linkages, States, Disruptions, Catalysts, Indicators, and the Navigation Process that integrates them. In Part 2, we will review each element in detail and provide specific language and distinctions that link each part to the whole.

Each of the core elements offers a specific way to assess and view a team or organization, from its most basic operations to the innovation of new lines of business or self-imposed disruptions.

At this level what is most important to remember is that each of these elements are interconnected and interdependent on each other within a context of continuous change. Changing one will, by definition, have an impact (whether intended or unintended) on each of the others.

Summary

Every team and organization exists in its own Complexity Space™, comprised of interconnected internal and external Ecosystems. This is precisely why this work is as much about developing comfort with new ways of seeing, talking about and doing change as it is about accomplishing goals.

As you move forward these three concepts serve as the foundation for all that follows:

- Complexity science informs organizational change in a different way than traditional change models

- Patterns give form and function to the dynamics in an organization

- Both Red Lens and Blue Lens perspectives are always present and always interconnected

Part 2: Complexity Space™ Framework

The whole is comprised of (and is sometimes greater than) the sum of its parts.

Reinforcing one of the major themes of this book, each of the CSF elements is infinitely complex in its own right, and even more complex in combination. Although each is highly distinctive, we have identified universal aspects of each that offer enough structure and consistency to provide resilience and stability.

We may not be able to provide a part-by-part blueprint for building, operating and navigating the connections throughout an organization, but we have identified "Meta Patterns" that are found across organizational systems and span the core elements of the Complexity Space™ Framework.

There are four overlapping Meta Patterns:

- Defining (Awareness) Patterns
- Action Patterns
- Traversing Patterns
- Event Patterns

Defining (Awareness) Patterns for seeing, understanding and developing the macro conditions for organizational change. They are represented by Dimensions (Ecosystem-wide Patterns) and States (strategic "Meta Patterns").

Action Patterns for developing tactical, adaptive, and agile approaches for continual assessment and response to behaviors and actions when implementing Pattern-based change. They are represented by Catalysts (actions for Pattern-based change) and Indicators (Pattern movements).

Traversing Patterns for navigation and linkage within an internal Ecosystem and between external Ecosystems. They are represented by Linkages and the Navigation Process.

We have also defined episodic **Event Patterns** called Disruptions, which highlight critical points for evaluating, responding to, or making major internal or external pattern shifts.

In Part 1, we provided the history and context that resulted in the creation of the Complexity Space™ Framework. We now turn our attention to providing a more detailed description of the CSF's various elements:

Complexity Space Framework

- Ecosystem(s)
- Dimensions
- Linkages
- States
- Disruptions
- Catalysts
- Indicators
- Navigation Process

Ecosystem(s) - Patterns in Context

The fish can't (usually) see the ocean it is swimming in.

Within the Complexity Space™, it is our belief that complex systems always exist within a context. That context both shapes, and is shaped by, a number of variables. Those variables influence the patterns of behavior of those interacting within that complex system.

The behavior of fish swimming 100,000 feet below the surface of the ocean – with its intense pressure and total darkness, is very different than a school of fish making its way through light-filled, extremely shallow waters. Fish that thrive in one of those contexts are likely to struggle in the other. Major disruptions within that context can have catastrophic implications for every element of the system.

We have chosen to name this organizing principle (concept) "Ecosystem(s)."

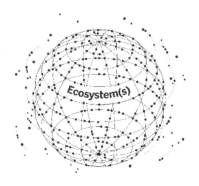

In our view, all Ecosystems share the following properties:

- Always present
- Operate at multiple layers simultaneously
- Not immediately visible
- Not predictably influenced
- Inputs/outputs not proportional
- Exists in the context of a particular place and point in time
- Open to external systems

Each of these properties allows us to focus on the nuances and distinctions in an Ecosystem's patterns.

Always present. Every team; every organization cannot help but exist within a context. By its very nature, it is impossible for a complex system to exist in a vacuum. For example, an established organization could be characterized by its rich history and tradition, while a startup might be characterized by its lack of those same properties.

Operates at multiple layers simultaneously. One of the properties that accounts for complexity in organizations is the fact that there is never "just one" Ecosystem. Every individual brings his or her unique history to their team or organization. Every team has its own unique story that both encompasses and is distinct from the team members that comprise it. Departments both encompass and are distinct from the teams that comprise them. Functions both encompass and are distinct from the departments that comprise them, and so on. There is continuous interaction between all of them, all of the time.

Not immediately visible. Like the fish in the quote that opens this section, the characteristics of these Ecosystems are not usually immediately known, accessible, discussed, or acted upon. In many cases, this is perfectly okay - these properties are taken for granted and the system goes about the work of accomplishing its desired goals. Failure to take these properties into account can be critical, though, when internal change is desired or external disruption requires change to occur within the system.

Not predictably influenced. Imagine your task is to clean up one square yard of water in the middle of the ocean. No sooner would you screen or process that water then it would be changed – tides, winds, fish swimming by, and your own actions would influence your desired area of change. Stories abound of organizations that invest massive resources in attempting to change their culture, only to find those efforts created unintended consequences that moved the system farther from its desired direction.

Inputs /outputs not proportional. Another property of Ecosystems is that they are persistent; often resisting change. We all know stories of organizations that have struggled to reinvent themselves when changes in technology or competitors have demanded it. In other cases, what appear to be small changes "go viral," creating impacts that far outweigh the original triggering event.

Exists in the context of a particular place and point in time. Complex systems are always evolving, always emerging. In fact, continuous change is a condition for complex systems survival. Without the continuous beating of our hearts, expansion and contraction of our lungs, shedding of old skin cells and the growing of new, human beings cannot survive. The continuous acquisition and integration of data, knowledge, and experience generated from both inside and outside the organization results in something that is different from even a moment before. These differences may be very subtle or might be profound - it is not possible to know with certainty where on that continuum the next changes will occur.

Open to external systems. A complex system is healthiest when it receives and responds to continuous internal and external feedback. When a system is open to other systems, all are beneficiaries of new and diverse exchanges of information, data, and innovations. If the system is closed off from these exchanges, over time it becomes unable to adequately interact with and respond to its surrounding environments.

Dimensions - Ecosystem-Wide Patterns

Dimensions

While all Ecosystems share common properties, individual Ecosystems are uniquely differentiated by four "Dimensions" that represent (hold) specific and foundational Ecosystem-wide patterns. We believe that naming these Dimensions and their distinct patterns is critical. They allow all who are interested in organizational change to have a shared language with which to discuss, assess, and identify potential actions that would influence both team and organizational Ecosystems in support of desired Pattern-based change.

The four Dimensions we have identified are:

- History
- Context
- Culture
- Motivation

History. Every organization has a past. It may comprise a span of hundreds of years, or a matter of moments. Even in the case of a startup, the organization is born based on the past histories of those who founded it. That history can be something to be proud of – or something to be overcome. It can be a history of profitable enterprise – or one of poor decisions and economic ruin. In some cases, the past may include a rebirth – when the organization ceased to exist in its current form and, like a phoenix, "rose from the ashes" to reconstitute itself in a more adaptive form.

Context [Eco-subsystems]. As noted in the properties of Ecosystems above, complex systems cannot and do not exist in a vacuum. Each exists in a variety of linked Ecosystems, each of which contains its own unique set of characteristics. Surrounding or linked Ecosystems include (but are not limited to):

- Political
- Economic
- Technology
- Competitor
- Customer
- Regulatory

Political Eco-subsystem. In the United States, a democratically-led Congress has different priorities and policies then a Republican-led Congress.

Economic Eco-subsystem. Is the economy expanding? Contracting? Is money easy to obtain, or is it difficult? What are global exchange rates? Is it cheaper to do business in an organization's home country, or should it invest outside?

Technology Eco-subsystem. What hardware, software, networks, and unique combinations of those are available for use by teams or organizations at any given period of time? Before electricity, farming took place by way of horse, oxen, and human sweat labor. The advent of gasoline and the Industrial Revolution enabled tractors and combines. Advances in chemistry enabled the creation and use of chemical fertilizers and weed/pest suppression. Advances in weather forecasting enabled particular strategies for planting and harvesting crops, etc.

Competitor Eco-subsystem. An organization that functions without competition will do business differently than one facing fierce and multiple competitors. The marketing book, *"Blue Ocean Strategy"* by W. Chan Kim and Renée Mauborgne captures the differences in these Ecosystems.

It is also important to recognize that an organization's Ecosystem may change as new competitors enter the marketplace. Depending on the amount of time that has passed and the power of the competitor, this can have catastrophic implications for an organizational system. Imagine you are a taxi cab driver working in a city where Uber or Lyft have just been introduced. What stays the same? What would be different?

Customer Eco-subsystem. One major reason organizations and systems exist is to serve their customers. Organizations serving a narrow, homogeneous customer base function differently than those catering to a large and diverse customer base. This Ecosystem is also sensitive to the savvy and knowledge of the customer base. Looking at an organization's history and context over time often shows a major disruption created by greater access to information offered by the Internet, and greater public scrutiny offered by social media.

Regulatory Eco-subsystem. Global or multinational organizations often feel the impact of this Ecosystem most keenly. One division of a corporation may be working in the United States, with relatively lower levels of regulation, while a second division is located in China, where regulatory restrictions are very high. Within a single geography, the finance subsystems are likely to be working in a more highly regulated Ecosystem than the marketing function. At an even more granular level, within any one department, one manager's internal processes and preference for control may be very different than another manager's.

Culture. We struggled with the use of this word. It means something different to everyone. Yet the word is used so often when describing organizations, we felt it was important to include. Our operational definition of culture is *the way we view and do things around here,* or *that constellation of artifacts, stories, and formal and informal structures and processes that influences the behavior of individuals and groups when no one is watching.* It is often manifested in the behavior of the senior and powerful formal and informal leaders of the organization. Regardless of any written values statement or signed Code of Ethics, members of organizations look for clues in the actions – or as importantly, lack of actions – of their managers.

Motivation. Teams and organizations come into existence for a reason. Those reasons vary widely, ranging from providing a product or service at the highest quality or lowest price, solving a problem, providing an opportunity to support/learn/work/play with like-minded people, to making the world a better place. These are sometimes (but not always) documented through vision or mission statements, charters, or value propositions.

These *raison d'êtres* can (but don't always) provide motivation and purpose for team and organizational members. They explicitly or implicitly influence priorities and decision making. Disruptions to this purpose – whether initiated from within the organization or from changes in other Ecosystems – can change organizational dynamics in a significant way. The Pixar movie, "*Happy Feet,*" where an individual penguin feels compelled to dance, eventually changes the behavior of the entire flock.

All four Dimensions are always present, always interacting with each other, and always changing. Understanding them individually and collectively provides a powerful lens for understanding a complex system's past as well as its present condition.

An example may help illustrate this concept. Larry left external consulting to join Harley-Davidson as an internal OD consultant in 1989. The company was stabilizing after a tumultuous decade which included a leveraged buyout and being five hours away from bankruptcy in 1982. The workforce had experienced massive changes, with the York, Pennsylvania facility shrinking from a high of approximately 1800 employees in the late 1960s to a low of approximately 120 employees in the late 1970s. An aggressive turnaround manager, coupled with a keen emphasis on quality, innovation, and the engagement of employees helped return the census to approximately 1100 employees in the late 1980s.

It was fascinating to notice the difference between those employees who had been employed at Harley during the "bad old days" and those who had been more recently hired. New hires brought with them the rules and norms from their prior organizations. In assembly line work that often meant *"Don't work too hard - you'll make the rest of us look bad."* In those organizations, it was the role of managers and supervisors to maintain a focus on productivity and quality.

At Harley-Davidson, however, an employee on the assembly line producing sub-par work was more likely to be not-too-gently coached by a fellow employee to raise their quality standards. Those veteran employees had experienced first-hand the impact on themselves and their co-workers of poor quality and they were not about to let those reductions in force happen again.

To end this section where it began:

The fish can't (usually) see the ocean it is swimming in...

But it can choose where and how it swims.

Linkages – Connecting Patterns

Linkages

We define "Linkages" as the critical connections within and between Ecosystems and their Eco-subsystems. We have identified some characteristics of Linkages that enable shared conversation, assessment, prioritization, and potential ways to influence (build, reinforce and deploy across structural patterns in the Ecosystem) them:

- Rigidity/Permanence
- Visibility/Immediacy
- Scope/Span

Rigidity/Permanence. A massive, permanent fixture like the George Washington Bridge in New York City required tremendous planning, resources, and commitment to construct. It was built to be impervious to short-term changes – to withstand high winds, strong rains, hurricanes, and earthquakes as well as the millions of tons of traffic that cross it each day. That rigidity and permanence is both appropriate and necessary for it to function – so long as the island of New York does not shift location due to a variation in the seismic plates under the earth. In that instance, the bridge's inability to flex could create its downfall.

Contrast that with a temporary bridge erected after an earthquake occurs. The recognition here is that the ground may continue to shift and so the amount of flexibility (as compared to the degree of rigidity) engineered into the bridge is much higher and the assumption of permanence is much lower.

Visibility/Immediacy. Some of the vehicles for transitioning within and between Ecosystems may be more visible or obvious to the members of the team or organization than others. Creating a new organizational structure – for example, shifting the engineering function from a functional to business-line structure, is very obvious to all involved. Few are surprised when organizational charts change.

Other Linkages are less obvious. Over time, the stories told by influencers throughout the organization might shift in terms of their tone and emphasis. Gradual shifts in demographics and psychographics begin to change the nature of the workforce itself. Reporting relationships change. People are physically moved to new office locations within the organization.

Scope/Span. Linkages vary in the amount of traffic they can hold. A "fat pipe" in the world of data transmission denotes the ability to transfer a lot of information at one time. A 10 lane bridge allows more traffic to move in a given amount of time than a two lane bridge. It can be tempting to assume that a "fat pipe" is always desirable – and that is not always the case. What happens if the fat pipe crashes? What if a virus is introduced into all those bytes of information? When rescuing someone who has fallen through the ice in a lake, a small, light person usually brings a thin rope to the person they are trying to rescue. To do anything else is to increase the risk that the rescuer would fall through the ice as well.

Combining these different properties of Linkages enables an infinite number of ways to move within and between Ecosystems. The following examples illustrate these concepts.

Chris brings her own personal Ecosystem to a meeting of a club she is interested in potentially joining. She has no direct history with the club, although she has heard good things about it. She attends as a visitor, with no internally or externally generated obligation to join – or even attend another meeting. Both the club and Chris are "checking each other out." This initial meeting is a "thin pipe," a temporary Linkage between these two Ecosystems.

A new cohort of 24 volunteer firefighters begins their 6 months of initial training. Each individual within the cohort has made a significant commitment of time, learning, and physical preparation before the training even begins. As they go through the training together, their need to work together as a team for their individual and mutual safety will be emphasized over and over again.

This link is wider – 24 people going through the experience together. Some parts of the Linkage are very visible – the classes. Some parts are fairly permanent – the curriculum remains constant over time to assure each firefighter knows what s/he needs to know. The camaraderie, the "esprit de corps," evolves underground, over time, not visible to the naked eye. Yet each individual firefighter can always make the decision to leave the training without significant penalty.

Bob is convicted for 1st degree murder and sentenced to life in prison without the possibility of parole. This is an example of a permanent, one-way Link. While it is extremely visible to Bob – and will be for the rest of his life – once incarcerated, his presence there and the notoriety of his crime will gradually disappear. The once highly visible Linkage will become invisible.

These Linkages occur between:

- Individuals and other individuals
- Individuals and teams
- Teams and other teams
- Teams and departments
- Individuals and departments, ad infinitum

One particular mechanism for linking various elements of a complex system deserves special notice here – Learning.

In the authors' early conversations, we described the process of "Complex Adaptive Learning" (CAL). CAL recognizes that in Complex Adaptive Systems, what is "true" can change. How many planets are in our solar system? Are eggs good for you to eat?

Instead, CAL focuses on the process of learning – acquiring data, integrating it with what is already known, identifying and prioritizing opportunities that may arise from that integration, and defining and implementing appropriate actions as a result.

We went on to acknowledge that the CAL process itself is an Ecosystem, impacted by its own Ecosystem Dimensions and contextual Eco-subsystems. One individual's history of learning is different than another's. One organization's philosophy and approach to learning and professional development is different than another's.

Changes in situation (context) can amplify or discourage learning or knowledge transfer. For example, how eager would you be to share your 30 years of professional experience with the person who is replacing you due to your being laid off?

In the next section, we will explore the concept of "States" – different Meta Patterns exhibited by teams and organizations within the context of their Ecosystems that provide insight about their current aspirations, priorities, and patterns of thought and behavior.

States - Strategic "Meta Patterns"

States

Another way to characterize Ecosystems is by their intent – their "State." Some organizations work hard to stay the same; to maintain the **Status Quo**. Other teams and organizations have as their goal to change the status quo; pursuing **Innovation** – making evolutionary changes to better cope with internal or external needs for change. Yet other organizations challenge themselves to create revolutionary change – inventing something new; a brand-new paradigm, a new suite of products, services, or technology. We've named this third set of objectives **Mutation**.

It can be useful to visualize these three States in two different ways. The first arrays the three States along a horizontal axis:

Status Quo   Innovation   Mutation

Each of these States can be differentiated according to two properties:

- Amount or intensity of change
- Amount of time required to introduce change

Amount or intensity of change. Since the goal of the Status Quo state is no change, effort is expended to try to prevent it. A global brewing company invests phenomenal resources to produce consistent tasting beer over time and across bottling facilities. They attempt to source their raw materials from the same locations, using the agricultural tools available to them to create the most consistent set of materials possible. Variation is controlled in mechanical processes, while highly skilled tasters make minute adjustments so the taste of their light beer stays similar from bottle to bottle, lot to lot, and country to country.

In the Innovation state, the intent is to create some amount of change, so the severity or intensity of the change must be greater. Another brewing company creates seasonal brews. This provides them with a marketing advantage; the opportunity to talk about new ingredients and new opportunities to keep the brand "top of mind." These seasonal brews are introduced in addition to their standard offering. If all of the beers tasted the same, this approach would not work.

Nano- and micro-breweries have staked out the Mutation part of the continuum. A craft brewer combines chocolate and peanut butter flavors, while others have introduced exotic fruits, vegetables, spices, and brewing techniques to offer customers a totally different beer drinking experience.

Amount of time required to introduce change. For a team or organization whose goal is to stay the same, the rate at which any required change is introduced would ideally be slow and steady. The Ecosystem would reward "not rocking the boat." The dynamic is also encapsulated in the question, *How do you turn an ocean liner? Very slowly and carefully.*

This can be contrasted most visibly to the other end of the continuum – Mutation. Compared to an ocean liner, the competitive advantage of a water ski is its ability to stop, start, and turn on a dime. For water ski enthusiasts, this is what makes the sport so exciting – and so dangerous. The risk is high that operators pushing the envelope on their water ski will fall off. Somewhere between those two is the appropriate rate of change for systems operating in the Innovation state.

A second way to view the three States is as a pie chart.

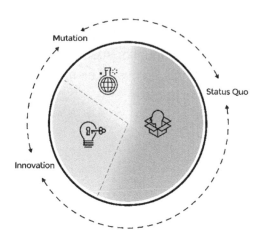

This visual provides a more nuanced message. It acknowledges that at any point in time, some parts of the system desire Status Quo, other parts seek evolutionary Innovation, while other parts seek revolutionary Mutation.

Characterizing the relative amounts of investment, energy, and resources dedicated to maintaining these states provides a powerful assessment tool for teams and organizations. It also creates a conversation for possibility: *Is where we are right now where we want or need to be in the future?* To the extent the answer to that question is "yes," the Ecosystems operate one way. To the extent the answer to the question is "no," it is a signal that something needs to be different.

We are presented daily with any number of current social, economic or political events which illustrate how quickly the conditions in complex systems can perturb even the most traditional and established industries and institutions. As we will explore in the Disruptions section, the circumstances for changes in States can be large or small, internally or externally generated, gradual or sudden. Each has the potential to shift patterns across all elements of the Ecosystem to varying degrees.

Disruptions – Disturbing Patterns

Disruptions

As we looked more deeply into this phenomenon, we recognized that there must be some mechanism; some trigger to create awareness that the current State does not serve the system today or will not serve the team or organization in the future. In the context of the three States, we have named these triggers "Disruptions."

We came to understand that Disruptions, like the States themselves, can be characterized across several different characteristics that help more fully describe them as well as provide insights as to the best way to address them:

- Proactive versus Reactive
- Internal versus External
- Intensity
- Duration of Disruption

Proactive versus Reactive. As a result of strategic planning, an organization might choose to expand its product line. This would be an example of a proactive disruption – the organization initiating a change in emphasis from one State to another. Conversely, an acquisition might provoke a reactive response in the acquired company.

Internal versus External. While the proactive versus reactive distinction focuses primarily on the intentionality of the Disruption, the internal versus external distinction focuses primarily on where the impetus for the Disruption originated. Did the organization create the Disruption as a result of implementing its strategic plan, or as a result of a new competitor?

Intensity. "The shot across the bow" or "the canary in the coal mine" are phrases that illustrate that certain Disruptions are small in nature. They are the "weak signals" that something may be getting ready to change. There is a sense of looking into the future to discern the significance of a weak Disruption.

A major natural disaster such as a major earthquake illustrates a very severe Disruption. The shock to the current State is violent, and significant. Action is typically needed immediately, with damage control often being the objective. It should be noted, though, that some Ecosystems view these intense Disruptions differently – as opportunities to move quickly to take advantage of the Disruption. This approach is captured in the phrase, *never waste a good crisis.*

Duration of the Disruption. In much the same way as proactive vs. reactive and internal versus external overlap, intensity and duration exhibit a similar overlapping quality. Global warming is a disruption that occurs a little bit at a time over a long period of time. A new trend in women's fashion, though, may burst on the scene with exposure in social media or through a celebrity factor, prompting clothing manufacturers to react quickly to "catch the wave." A Disruption could be slow and relatively low intensity, or slowly reach a crescendo of high intensity. Likewise, some Disruptions can happen very quickly, yet not move the intensity needle very much, while others are fast and relatively catastrophic.

"Both/And" characterizes the interdependence of these four characteristics of Disruptions. Each enables the opportunity for shared conversation and assessment:

- How internal/external, intense, and fast/slow are our current Disruptions?

- What characteristics do we need to change in order to help us survive and thrive in the continuously changing context we are dealing with in our particular Ecosystem?

The answers to those questions can inform both short- and long-term change strategies for teams and organizations.

Catalysts - Actions for Pattern-Based Change

Catalysts

In Part 1 we suggested that complexity-generated patterns in human systems have always existed. One reason why they were not integrated into the development of 20th century management theory and practice (Frederick Taylor's work) had to do with the prevailing knowledge and science available for understanding and making sense of human behavior and capacity.

In much the same way that physical and life sciences delivered new knowledge, materials, products and processes for accomplishing the seemingly impossible, the social and information sciences have provided us with a similar set of new knowledge, research, methodologies and networks for working with the distinctions between what we perceive as unmoving and linear but in reality are nonlinear and in-motion patterns.

The necessity of keeping a "Both/And" perspective is particularly relevant to deciding which lens to use for seeing and working with patterns – are they static or in motion? Is the current State a good fit for where the team or organization needs to be today? In the future? In the Complexity Space™ Framework, we use "Catalysts" when action is needed to influence Pattern-based change.

Properties and Types of Catalysts

The first step in using Catalysts is understanding their distinguishing properties as levers for Pattern-based change. Each Ecosystem component has the opportunity to influence the resilience, robustness and agility of any activity in the organization. However, it is the function of Catalysts to be the primary change stimulant for direct and intentional action.

Catalysts' unique attributes contribute to their effectiveness:

- Function across all elements of the CSF
- Operate at multiple layers simultaneously
- Offer alternatives for creating intentional shifts in patterns
- Can be modified directly, quickly and repeatedly
- Easily measured
- Generate shorter feedback cycles

To successfully integrate complexity-informed Catalysts into operations and decision making, we suggest building upon existing knowledge, skills, and tools that are familiar and readily available.

As we were developing the CSF, we described Catalysts as "levers" that people interested in influencing complex systems could push, pull and pivot to perturb the system's current patterns.

Although "levers" is a familiar mechanical term, we believe that the concept of a chess piece, specifically the queen, more accurately represents the act of making moves that create intentional shifts in patterns. The Queen, the icon we selected, is arguably the most powerful piece because it has the largest number of possible moves available to it.

We have intentionally limited our discussion of systems theory, however a principle called the Law of Requisite Variety (LRV) emphasizes the critical nature of Catalysts in complex systems. Variety equates to exploring different options for achieving a goal or operation. Proactively seeking new knowledge and new approaches to accomplish a goal introduces a mindset of flexible, adaptive and creative practices.

In the Complexity Space™ Framework, the dynamics of Ecosystems continually generate changing contexts that suggest being ready for when doing the same procedure no longer produces the same result.

As we think about the Law of Requisite Variety and Catalysts as chess pieces, we should anticipate that our moves will generate the occasional unexpected response. Again, we'd like to reinforce that Catalysts are designed to perturb patterns – with no guarantee that you'll get the results you intend.

There is no guarantee that the patterns will shift, or that change will occur in a desired, predicted way. Rather, the hope is that they will shift in *some* way – and that those shifts can be assessed, discussed, learned from, and serve as the basis for the next informed action. In this section we focus on the specific language and distinctions for utilizing Catalysts.

The seven types of Catalysts should be both familiar and recognizable – they have been used by organizations in some way or the other to drive change for a long time. The distinction is how they operate to stimulate pattern shifts across the Ecosystem.

The seven Catalysts for Pattern-Based Change in Ecosystems are:

- Connections
- Leadership
- Stories
- Risk Taking
- Organizational Structures
- Systems
- Processes

Each of these Catalysts is purposely left open to a wide range of diverse and emergent applications (models etc.). You will notice there is an overlap between the categories. This is intentional – in fact, consistent with the properties of Complex Adaptive Systems, intervening in any one of these Catalysts will by definition, have some sort of impact on each of the others.

Connections. When we speak of Connections, we are referring to "the relationships and linking of existing and potential intersections of people, ideas, resources, structures and patterns within and between Ecosystems." For example, a department manager could arrange a "meet and greet" with another department. At one of Larry's clients, facility leaders were encouraged to walk the shop floor each week, looking specifically to initiate contacts with people they did not yet know.

Leadership. We define Leadership as, "practiced formal and informal roles within an organization's Ecosystem for accountability, authority, decision making, risk taking and innovation." For example, rotating leadership assignments will perturb the usual patterns of leader/follower in some way. Another of Larry's clients instituted a "Six Sigma Olympics," where groups of employees were encouraged to band together to find and fix problems on their own.

Stories. We define Stories as, "the intuitive and emotional formation of institutional narratives and experiences that link individual and group behaviors contextually to the organization." We know that stories are one of the most efficient and powerful ways to create emotion – one of the most powerful motivators for change.

Consider the statement, *Think about a time you lost one of your most precious possessions.* Very few people will experience a positive emotion. Yet in that one sentence, each of us will likely access something deep and powerful that results in the sad feeling the author intends. Are your "change stories" focused on opportunity or threat? Risk or reward?

Risk Taking. Our view of Risk Taking is, "creating and embracing differences in every aspect of the organization for learning, experimenting, failing, assessing and disrupting."

One of the dynamics of moving between the Status Quo and the other States is increased risk. This is a result of moving from the known to the unknown.

How does your team or organization react when something does not work according to plan? Do you "shoot the messenger?" Figure out who to blame? Unfortunately, many teams and organizations *say* that failure is OK, but then punish (explicitly or implicitly; immediately or over time when it comes to promotions, etc.) those who do.

One of Larry's favorite stories was shared by the City Manager of Scottsdale, AZ. He instituted the "Turtle Award." A ceramic turtle was mounted on a small wooden base with a plaque that read, *Behold the turtle, who never got anywhere without sticking its neck out.* The Manager asked each member of his staff to nominate an employee who had made the most intelligent failure during the last month to receive the award, which was attended by the City Manager himself at one of the best restaurants in Scottsdale. Do you think he perturbed the pattern of risk taking? It worked!

Organizational Structures. We describe Organizational Structures as, "the composition and complex interrelationships of all the 'parts and assets' that comprise and define the organization's Ecosystem." Organizations change their organizational charts all of the time. We include this category of interventions as an Ecosystem Catalyst because of the changes in patterns it will engender.

New seating arrangements create different peer, "cubicle" conversations. New managers have different expectations (note the overlap with the "Leadership" catalyst). Hierarchical vs. matrixed vs. team-based structures – each offers its own patterns of interaction and decision making.

Systems. For us, Systems are "the interconnected network and technical frameworks that support the flow of information, knowledge, and social actions." *Knowledge is power.* Changing the quality, quantity, and accessibility of the information available will change the conversations that occur as employees strive to do their work.

It is not an accident that tools like Yammer and Lync are being rolled out to employees to provide easy access to other people from their ever-present cell phones. "Big data" initiatives attempt to capture and make sense of the mountains of raw data available, providing a different way to "see" trends.

Processes. We define Processes as, "continuous formal and informal sets of practices, policies, operational activities and procedures that offer resilience during continuous pattern changes". A mainstay of the Red Lens Paradigm is clearly defined, succinct, step-by-step processes that document the best way to perform a task. In mechanical systems aspiring to the Status Quo, they are often "true and useful."

In the Blue Lens Paradigm, we recognize that changing Process steps changes the patterns of interactions of those that execute that process. This paradigm also places a premium on Processes that are robust and adaptive.

Each of the Catalysts we have identified serve multiple purposes, sustaining and leveraging what is in place while making choices to proactively shift patterns and reactively respond to continuous outcomes. Catalysts are critical to building an adaptive practice of frequent lower risk actions (experiments) for generating results, engaging people for feedback, and co-creating proactive choices for the "next smart steps" which we will explain in the next section.

We repeatedly rely on versions of the following questions to prompt additional inquiry and new answers:

- If you are preparing to make a significant change in the organization's business model or structure, how will you use Catalysts to address existing and develop new tactical and adaptive drivers for the business?
- How do you talk about successful teams and their ways of operating with one another?
- What frameworks and technologies are used for employees to collaborate with one another?
- What systems and processes are in place to expedite innovation and change?
- How transparent and open are existing leadership practices and models to changes directed at leaders and managers?
- How do stories help you hear and see and understand a different *What would you do?*
- What are the networks (connections) that already exist and are effective or not?
- How could we support a wider range of experiments in all areas of the organization?
- Is the structure of the organization such that once slotted you never get to move elsewhere?
- Who is making waves in the organization? Who do we listen to?
- What are the stories we tell ourselves and our customers? What are the stories that have caused us to rethink our direction or strategy, etc.?

Next Smart Steps

We continue to emphasize that viewing teams or organizations through the Blue Lens Paradigm focuses attention on their constantly changing, self-organizing, sometimes unpredictable characteristics. It is impossible to prune a growing shrub and know with certainty exactly what it will look like 3 years in the future. The very act of pruning changes not just the trimmed branches, but the plant's utilization of nutrients, the amount of light hitting various parts of the plant, the potential for insects and disease, etc.

Experienced gardeners know this. They prune using a combination of science, experience, and hope. They usually prune sparingly at first, then notice the results. If the results are favorable, they do more of the same. If the results are not what is hoped for, they assess, learn – and do something different.

We have named the dynamic described above as taking the "next smart step." Smart steps recognize change agents' inability to control all of the variables at play in the Complexity Space™ Framework. What we *can* do is influence – to use our knowledge, experience, and intuition to perturb patterns and then pay keen attention to *all* of the consequences of the change we introduced – those we intended and those we didn't.

We often use the language of "trying experiments" to capture the humility and curiosity we think are essential for taking a "smart step" approach. Given all of the complexity, there is a very large likelihood that things will NOT go exactly as planned. That doesn't mean we failed – or that we picked the wrong Catalyst(s) – or that it was a "bad" intervention – or that we are bad change agents. Instead, to use one of Larry's favorite sayings, *There is no failure unless there is failure to learn.*

The concept of what "success" means changes depending on which paradigm – Red Lens or Blue Lens is being focused on. In the next section, we will explore that in our conversation about Indicators.

Indicators - Pattern Movements

Indicators

In the Complexity Space™ Framework, "Indicators" become the essential instruments for calibrating Pattern-shifting interventions while maintaining effective and robust operations.

How do I know it's working?   What difference did it make? These questions are critical to any business and any change agent. When resources (people, systems, money, etc.) are invested in making change and improvements happen, it is important to understand the "return on investment" for those expenditures.

In the Red Lens Paradigm, those measures and metrics are fairly well defined. They include:
- Quality
- Cost
- Timeliness
- Compliance
- Customer Satisfaction
- Employee Satisfaction & Engagement

We are confident that our readers are already familiar with these, so we provide only brief explanations and examples.

Quality. Six Sigma and other process improvement approaches focus on defect reduction. DPMO (Defects Per Million Opportunities) is one standard metric.

Cost. Calculated in dollars, hours, or productivity (output per unit of input). Did the product or service of interest cost more or less than we expected it to?

Timeliness. What business does not care about timeliness or responsiveness? The axiom, *Time is money* has been around for a long time – and with good reason. Are deadlines being met? Production rates being maintained?

Compliance. Rules. Regulations. Policies and procedures. Externally imposed by government or legislative bodies, or internally created, "breaking the rules" creates liability and hardship.

Customer satisfaction. Do customers stay? Do they recommend products and services to others? Do they purchase more?

Employee satisfaction and engagement. Do employees stay? Do they provide more effort and initiative than what is needed to not get fired?

Profit and Loss/Financial Metrics. Whether public or private, profit, loss, cash flow, inventory turns, etc. are considered by many stakeholders to be the ultimate outcome.

Each of these, individually and collectively, offer insight as to the outcome of any change investment. Notice, though, the emphasis on outcome. These measures focus more on *Did we catch a fish?* than *What was our process for fishing?* They are typically tangible in nature, and reasonably easy to see and measure. They are also easier to convert to the "dollars and cents" consequences that are of critical interest to accountants and stakeholders.

These measures and metrics are less helpful when trying to provide answers or insights about the extent and direction of Pattern-based change. Pattern-based change requires trying to measure something that is continuously changing and moving; measuring combinations of variables where past performance does not necessarily predict future performance.

Measuring Pattern-based change requires identifying "weak signals," the "canary in the coal mine;" the "leading indicators" of movement, self-organization, emergence, and other dynamic processes. Compared to Red Lens Paradigm metrics, Indicators are more forward looking and "softer" in nature – helping the observer to focus attention in a particular area of the Ecosystem.

We do not believe there is one single measure or metric that adequately describes all aspects of the Complexity Space™ Framework. Instead, we prefer to consider a "dashboard" of Indicators that taken together, offer some insights as to the present condition of the system and some intuition as to where it might be headed. Consider the following Indicators and inquiries:

1. **Awareness: Is there a difference?** Has the particular pattern of thought or behavior being focused on changed at all? Note there is no positive or negative value associated with the answer, except in the context of your intent. In complex systems like organizations, not every intervention will create discernable change.

2. **Direction: Is the difference helping to move towards, away from, or on a tangent from some desired outcome?** Assuming there is a difference, in what direction is it? Another of the properties of complex systems is there is no guarantee patterns will shift in desired ways. Sometimes "unintended consequences" are disastrous – other times, unexpectedly delightful.

3. **Velocity: Is the rate of difference increasing or decreasing?** If patterns are changing, at what rate? Is that rate constant? Relative to what?

4. Turbulence: How abrupt are the pattern changes?
Are they smooth or turbulent? Predicted or
unpredicted?

What remains the same? What is different? This inquiry
provides another way to look at the four Indicators above. It
acknowledges that within the myriad of linked Ecosystems
and States, *"It is all always there."* Some elements appear to
be stable, while others are moving in intended directions and
yet others are moving in tangential or unintended ways. As
contexts change and Disruptions occur, the answers to the
questions above can change rapidly and unpredictably.

How are relationships changing? This question focuses
attention on the Linkages. It invites a conversation about one
person's relationship to another person; an individual's
relationship to his or her team; one division's relationship
with another division; and so on.

Is learning taking place? This question allows insight into
how new knowledge is infiltrated throughout the
organization. We can look for what is changing in both
relevant internal and external contexts. Is learning:

- Intended and/or unintended?
- Formal and/or informal?
- Shared or hoarded?

Summary

As we developed the Complexity Space™ Framework, we realized that there is a symbiotic relationship between these Pattern-based Indicators and the Red Lens Paradigm's more finite, outcome-oriented measures and metrics. *If we change these patterns, with all of the intended and unintended ripples they will cause, ultimately at any one given point in time, quality, cost, timeliness, etc. will be impacted in some way – and not necessarily for the better.* Said differently, at the end of the day, the very best fishing techniques in the world will leave the fishermen hungry if they do not end up with a fish in their boat.

Having introduced the language and distinctions of the Complexity Space™ Framework, we can now begin to discuss how they interrelate and how they can be sequenced to provide guidance for those trying (beginning) to navigate in this new paradigm.

To provide context, we will begin the next section with a discussion of some of the most popular approaches currently in use within the Red Lens Paradigm. We will then show how we've extended the natural evolution of those models to one more specifically focused on Pattern-based change.

We will also provide a process that explains how a change agent might intentionally navigate and link the various elements of the CSF in pursuing a desired change.

The Navigation Process

Navigation Process

Returning to a recurring theme in the book (and this is a good thing!), the Red Lens Paradigm provides a number of researched and tested process guides – sequences of steps to help an individual, team, or organization move in a systematic way from their current state to a desired future state. Larry has personally helped teach and facilitate 3-step, 4-step, 6-step, 9-step, and 27(!)-step problem solving processes.

There are many processes for improving an organization's operation from the traditional management playbook. We share the following in large part because they are widely recognized and because we consistently integrate them in our work as appropriate:

- Six Sigma – DMAIC
- Lean Enterprise – PDCA
- Agile Development
- ADDIE

Recognizing the value and use of these models, especially if they are currently part of an organization's business strategy, establishes a shared perspective as we introduce and integrate the complementary benefits of the Complexity Space™ Framework "Navigation Process."

We share the key elements of each model below.

Six Sigma

Six Sigma, originated in the mid 1980's by Motorola and still popular today utilizes the "DMAIC" process.

Define. What is the scope of the problem to be addressed? Project charters and other tools are used to help sponsors and teams create projects that are big enough to provide a meaningful return on investment, yet bounded enough to be achievable with the resources and time available.

Measure. Develop a data-based, shared understanding of the current state. What is really going on? Process mapping is one of many tools that assist in this phase.

Analyze. Determine the root cause of the problem. Once we know why the problem is occurring, we can target specific corrective actions that not only solve the existing problem, but ideally prevent it from ever occurring again. Pareto Charts are one of the most popular tools.

Improve. Identify and implement the actions that will eliminate the root cause(s) of the problem. Pilots are a valuable tool.

Control. Establish mechanisms to assure the corrective actions become the "new normal." Establishing measures, metrics, and audits are powerful tools to assist in this phase.

Define → **Measure** → **Analyze** → **Improve** → **Control**

Notice the step-by-step approach. In rigorous Six Sigma applications, there are "phase gate" reviews with detailed checklists of steps to be followed and tools to be used before moving to the next phase. Implied is that if the team performs the steps properly, there should be no reason to move backwards in the process.

Lean

In the 1990s, John Womack adapted "Lean Enterprise" methodology from the Toyota Production System as a next generation of process improvement methodologies. Lean provides the "PDCA" process.

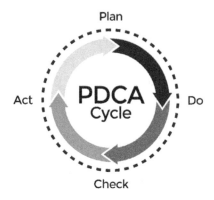

Plan. Create a hypothesis; an experiment which if successful, will reduce non-value added activity or improve flow and customer satisfaction. Value Stream Maps are a common tool.

Do. Conduct the experiment; implement the planned improvement. There are a host of Lean tools to support this phase.

Check. Evaluate the results of the efforts in the "Do" phase. Did they accomplish their desired effect? The emphasis here is on learning, assuming that whatever the result, there is more potential improvement possible.

Act. If the change is deemed successful and worth repeating, document and teach it to others so it becomes the new standard way the process should work. If it is not, the focus changes to maximizing the learning gained from the experience, which is then rolled forward into the next "Plan" phase as the cycle begins again.

Compared to DMAIC, the Lean process is more flexible. In particular, the "Check" phase of the process acknowledges that the actions performed in the "Do" phase may, or may not have achieved their desired outcome. If the actions were successful, the appropriate steps in the "Act" phase are to standardize them so they become the new "normal," the new standard process for all to follow. However, if the actions taken in the "Do" phase did not achieve their desired goal, the appropriate steps in the "Act" phase are to learn from what happened and "Plan" a new set of actions based on that learning.

Agile

In the early 2000s, "Agile" software development became popular in large part because new information, feedback and changes were intentionally and continually integrated into the project development process. This methodology extended the flexibility of PDCA even more.

We believe there is a lot to like about the Agile approach. It is consistent with many of the assumptions at the foundation of the Complexity Space™ Framework:

- Things change quickly and unpredictably

- Short feedback cycles create frequent opportunities for awareness, assessment, and learning

- Having diverse team members creates rich conversations to help the team be aware of the various Ecosystem Dimensions at play

Agile methods recognize several important aspects of project dynamics:

Customers change their minds. Traditional project management approaches ask customers to document their requirements, which are then turned into specifications and requirements. Code is written to meet these specs, with the customer having the opportunity to validate them during User Acceptance Testing (UAT). Developers are often upset if the customer says, *This is what I said I wanted, but now that I see it, I've changed my mind.* In Agile, the expectation is that the customer *will* change their mind as the development emerges.

Cross-functional teams that include customers. In top-down, "waterfall" development analysts create specs, then turn them over to programmers, who turn their results over to quality, who then turn it over to testers, who – finally – engage the end user. In Agile, representatives from each of those functions are present on the team, with their efforts coordinated by a facilitator ("Scrum Master").

Short "Sprints" of activity. Traditional, "we'll design the implementation from the first element to the last" mentality, results in long, involved, highly structured project plans which are great in theory – until the first major disruption or change in customer requirements. In Agile, all of the various ultimate deliverables are chunked into discrete pieces and placed in a Backlog. Each week or two, these are reviewed by a cross-functional team and the next, highest priority pieces are divided into two- to four-week segments of work.

"Minimum Viable Product." In Agile, the intended result of each Sprint is a "good enough to test with the customer" level product. Why create a polished final product, complete with documentation, only to find out the customer wants something else?

Daily "Huddles." Agile recognizes that the constantly changing and evolving development of software, hardware, and processes requires frequent communication. Daily Huddles – 10-15 minute stand-up meetings focus on three major questions:

1. Did we accomplish yesterday's tasks?
2. What is our plan for today?
3. What information do we need to share with each other, or what help do we need to request or offer, in order to accomplish the objectives of this Sprint within its charter and timeline?

ADDIE

The ADDIE development model continues the progression of recognizing the "change-ability" of a change process. ADDIE stands for **Analyze, Design, Develop, Implement, Evaluation.**

In the ADDIE graphic, notice that Evaluation is at the center of the development process, with revisions expected throughout.

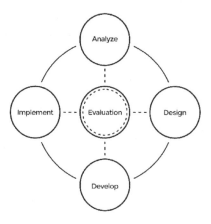

The CSF Navigation Process

The CSF Navigation Process integrates the approaches described in the previous sections by focusing on influencing patterns – patterns of development; patterns of experimentation; patterns of learning – the patterns of change.

As we will explain, the Navigation Process is a complex process in its own right, subject to the contextual factors and Disruptions always at play in a team or organization.

Graphically, we depict the Complexity Space™ Framework Navigation Process like a Network Diagram. In keeping with the "everything is connected to everything else" property of complex systems, it acknowledges that each phase interacts with every other phase.

The progression through the various elements of the CSF Navigation Process is often not linear. A Disruption could provoke a reactive crisis, causing the organization to retreat from its "best laid" plans, goals and objectives.

Notice as well that each of the seven steps of the Navigation Process are framed as questions. This is deliberate. Framing key points as questions is designed to invite inquiry and dialogue so the "next smart steps" can be defined.

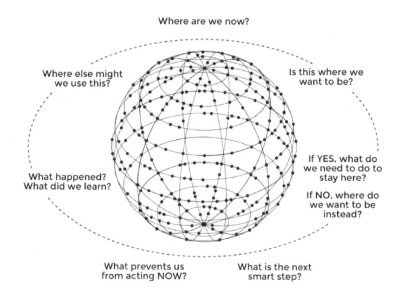

Where are we now?

Where else might we use this?

Is this where we want to be?

What happened?
What did we learn?

If YES, what do we need to do to stay here?

If NO, where do we want to be instead?

What prevents us from acting NOW?

What is the next smart step?

The CSF Navigation Process begins with a question common to the other approaches: **Where are we now?**

Teams or organizations are asked to engage in a reflection and dialogue about the past and current patterns of the various elements of the Complexity Space™ Framework relevant to their inquiry.

Sample questions include:

- How would we currently describe our History, Context, Culture, and Motivation?

- How would we describe our past and current States? To what extent are the various elements of our team and organization in each?

- What are the major Disruptions – internal and external – that made a significant impact on our past? What Disruptions are we experiencing now?

- How would we describe the Catalysts we used in the past? How did they work? Which ones are we using now? How are they working?

- How would we currently describe the Indicators (process, patterns, and outputs) we are using today? How well are they working?

The discussions provoked by these questions have several objectives. The obvious one is to gather the answers; the content. Equally important, these conversations begin the process of changing team and organizational patterns by changing the patterns of conversation!

In our experience, these topics of conversation are seldom, if ever, the primary areas of inquiry. Making them explicit allows the various participants in the conversations to discover:

- Where perceptions are similar and where they differ ("Same and Different")

- New information about people and history (*I didn't know you/the organization ...*)

- Insights about past and present contextual factors (*Given the technology and competitors present at the time ...*)

These insights serve as the foundation for the second step in the Navigation Process by exploring, *Is this where we want to be?* Will our current State enable us to survive and thrive in the present, near- and long-term future?" Note the terms "survive" and "thrive." We chose "survive" deliberately to heighten awareness of the dangers of assuming the current State, or percentage of resources invested in each of the various States, is correct.

We often use the question, How would you like to be the best 8-track recorder manufacturer in the world? to highlight the dangers of ignoring changes in the surrounding Ecosystem Dimensions.

The third step in the Navigation Process depends on the answer to the question, *Is this where we want to be?* If the team or organization is satisfied with its current State, strategies, and ability to survive and thrive, then the next question is, *If yes, what do we need to do to stay here?*

What do we need to do so we can continue to survive and flourish in the present and near- and long-term future? We chose "flourish" to sensitize participants in the conversation to the opportunities available if they are willing to proactively initiate change. This approach explicitly acknowledges the ever-changing nature of the internal and external Eco-subsystems in which the team or organization interacts.

An advantage of using the Navigation Process is that it forces attention both inward and outward, in the present and the future. It invites a conversation about contingency planning and risk management. Attention is paid to the Catalysts, with a focus on which of them may need to be leveraged in order to maintain the current, desired State.

If the answer to the question, *Is this where we want to be?* is "no," the third question changes to, *If no, where do we want to be instead?* If we want/need to be different than we are today, what is our desired State? Simply to say different than where we are now does not provide sufficient guidance. This is reinforced by the popular maxim, *If you don't know where you're going, how will you know when you arrive?* This question is intended to create inquiry and dialogue to determine the future direction/State of the team or organization. The answer will be informed by conversations about relevant Ecosystems and Dimensions; about vision, mission, and strategy, about available resources, and a host of other topics.

Regardless of the decision to maintain the current State or move to a different desired State, the fourth question in the Navigation Process is the same. *What is the next smart step?* Again, the language here is chosen carefully. In the Complexity Space™ Framework, we acknowledge there is no one, guaranteed, best way to manage or control all of the variables in a Complex Adaptive System. Instead, the Navigation Process invites participants to think about "the next smart step" – an intervention; an experiment designed to perturb the existing patterns – hopefully in the desired direction.

These experiments/interventions should be carefully planned and designed to maximize their learning value. Using tools from the Red Lens Paradigm is encouraged – indeed, necessary, to focus attention on what Catalyst(s) to influence, what Ecosystem Dimensions to monitor, and what Indicators are needed.

Once planned, the fifth step in the Navigation Process is, *What prevents us from acting NOW?* The "NOW" in the question serves to emphasize the need for action. An attribute of complex systems is that it is impossible to have perfect and complete knowledge of them due to their constantly being in flux. This is either bad or good news depending on your point of view.

The bad news: Change is risky! Change agents are susceptible to the charge of acting recklessly. If only we had collected more data … We should have anticipated this … are typical "Monday morning quarterback" phrases when organizational changes don't achieve their desired results.

To avoid this risk, teams seek more data, often resulting in "analysis paralysis." It is a safe, politically correct strategy – that results in no change at all, or small, slow, and safe change – which ultimately may not impact the patterns needed for adaptive and sustainable change.

The good news: recognizing that having complete and accurate information is unrealistic – indeed impossible – enables a different approach to Pattern-based change. The "null hypothesis" in the classic scientific method states there will not be a statistically significant change.

Said differently, our default position is the proposed change won't work! If it does create significant change, classic science states the conclusion that we disproved the null hypothesis this time – and future experiments should seek to replicate and build on this result. Notice how the emphasis shifts to learning rather than a given outcome.

When a Pattern-changing intervention/experiment is implemented, the sixth step, *What happened? What did we learn?* phase of the Navigation Process naturally follows.

The Complexity Space™ Framework enables change agents to implement their ideas with a sense of curiosity rather than dread; with emphasis on process and patterns as well as specific results; with recognition that the results – good or bad – are simply data and not someone's "fault."

It is similar to the "Check" phase of Lean's PDCA cycle in noticing the results of the change that was implemented in the "Do" phase.

It is also consistent with central role of Evaluation in the ADDIE development model.

The CSF Navigation Process further extends this emphasis on noticing and learning by focusing on Pattern-based change:

- Is there any?
- How much?
- In what direction?
- What are the intended and unintended impacts on other patterns?

The Navigation Process uses questions like these to provoke dialogue – ideally throughout the team or organization – in both formal and informal ways. This has the advantage of not only maximizing the learning about the impact of the intervention/experiment on Pattern-based change, but actually serves as another Catalyst in its own right.

What better way to create or evolve employee engagement than to invite the members of the Ecosystem to "go to the observation deck," away from their daily tasks, to become students of their own team and organization.

The final question of the Navigation Process, is *Where else might we use this?* One of the key properties of patterns is that while the specifics may vary, their overall properties remain fairly consistent over time and varying conditions. Where do similar patterns exist? Might some adaptation of the Pattern-shifting behavior add value in other places?

Summary

Let's throw a bunch of ideas against the wall and see what sticks is typically seen as an ineffective, inefficient way to make change happen. Systematic approaches like DMAIC and PDCA evolved in the Red Lens Paradigm to provide step-by-step processes to follow in pursuit of continuous improvement and change. More recently, Agile and ADDIE approaches recognized ongoing change through their more interactive approaches to project success.

We have attempted to provide specific language and distinctions that invite increased awareness and the opportunity for more nuanced conversations for looking at organizational patterns through the lenses of the Complexity Space™ Framework.

The CSF Navigation Process further extends this acknowledgment of complexity, assuming that self-organization, interdependence, evolution, and mutation will render rigid plans obsolete very quickly. Focusing on patterns, it is constructed as a series of questions, the results of which will create purposeful conversations and experiments.

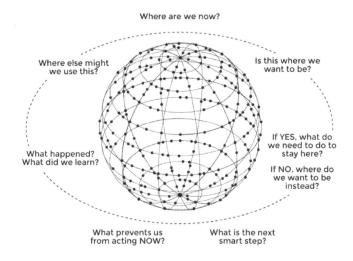

Where are we now?

Where else might we use this?

Is this where we want to be?

If YES, what do we need to do to stay here?

If NO, where do we want to be instead?

What happened? What did we learn?

What prevents us from acting NOW?

What is the next smart step?

Where are we? What should we try? What did we learn? Where else might we use this? These questions focus attention on underlying patterns that provide greater leverage for change than one-time fixes.

Each component offers its own set of Pattern-based language. From here, we hope it leads to curiosity about how each component is playing out in your specific situation. We hope that curiosity leads to assessment, reflection, experimentation, and learning.

If you give someone a fish they eat for a day. If you teach them to fish, they eat for a lifetime.

Part 3: Applying the Complexity Space™ Framework

In Part 3, we bring the concepts, models, and tools of the Complexity Space™ Framework to "Ground Zero" as change agents tasked with helping a complex organization make progress on a "sticky issue."

We will first provide a somewhat detailed "blow by blow" description of the process that began with our engagement and continued through the completion of the project. Consistent with our "teach them how to fish" mindset, we focus on the process and dynamics rather than the particular content which may not be relevant to anyone else.

Once we have described what happened, we will revisit the case, relating it to the various elements of the Complexity Space™ Framework. We will focus that commentary at two different levels – how it informed our thinking as designers of the change intervention and how it impacted the client's possibilities for new thought and action in pursuit of their goals.

Before you read the case we have a confession – it will seem messy – because it is! We are not sharing this case to look good. We had a plan and had to revise it, not because we wanted to but because that's what happens in complex change. The challenge we faced was how to balance adhering to our carefully designed and client-centric plan with the data and conditions that emerged during the project. The case presents an unfiltered view of how to utilize the Complexity Space™ Framework.

Complexity Space Framework

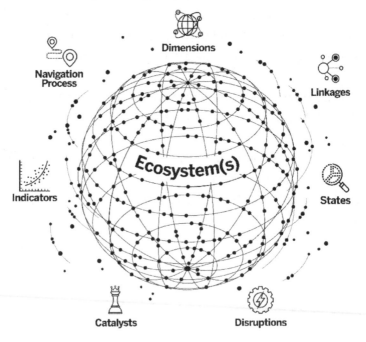

Dimensions

Navigation Process

Linkages

Indicators

Ecosystem(s)

States

Catalysts

Disruptions

Financial Services Case Study

Larry was approached by a client with whom he'd worked a number of years before. The request was to facilitate a strategic planning session for their financial services company. To maintain confidentiality, we'll call them FSC (Financial Services Company).

FSC was founded in the early 1990s by several financial planners who were frustrated by their current employer, a major insurance company.

FSC began by offering fee-based financial planning and estate services. The business grew organically, with each of the founding partners leveraging their networks, making cold calls, and using referrals to expand the business. With the growth, they added services (money management), staff, and new offices.

As the firm continued to grow, the partners invested in technology to better manage operations and client services. They also focused on public relations and expanding their social media presence. Partners emphasized speaking and leadership roles at relevant national and international professional association conferences.

As the level of organic growth began to slow, FSC began to re-think its value proposition. It added third party support services for other, smaller financial planning firms and began a series of acquisitions. A major investment in technology was considered necessary to enable the business to reach its next level of long-term profitability.

All of this change created confusion about how to prioritize and allocate resources between the various goals and investments that had been made. FSC leaders realized they would benefit from an outside presence to keep their conversations focused and productive. After an unsuccessful search for a local facilitator, the partners remembered their prior successful work with Larry and requested his facilitation services.

Responding to the Initial Request

Larry's initial reaction was to clarify the desired outcome of the work. Was it really just facilitation, or was something more required? The original request was to provide assistance for a one-day offsite meeting, which was eventually expanded to two days.

Larry shared the request with Denise during one of their regularly scheduled conversations. Denise immediately shared that she had facilitated a similar conversation for a client in the financial services sector a short time before. This prompted an inquiry by Larry to FSC to determine if they would be interested in a second consultant. They agreed and Denise became part of the process at that point.

For the remainder of this section, we will describe at a high level the phases of this project. We will then provide commentary as seen through the interactions between the Red Lens and Blue Lens perspectives. These conversations are not meant to be exhaustive and complete; but rather to give the reader an idea of how each lens, individually and together, informed our decision making in supporting FSC.

In order to increase readability, we describe what happened in each project phase, followed by paragraphs that describe relevant perspectives from the Red Lens and Blue Lens Paradigms. In our minds, though, we think of them as equally important and valuable.

Even our earliest conversations and initial assessment of the project were filtered through both lenses, which immediately suggested designing a plan that could be adapted in real time.

Red Lens Perspective

Adapting questions from newspaper journalism, Larry probed for the "Who, What, Where, When, and Why" of the request. Questions derived from the Lean Six Sigma body of knowledge were asked, particularly around "Voice of the Customer" and what a successful outcome would look like. *What is the fish you need to catch today?*

Blue Lens Perspective

The preliminary conversations made it very obvious there were larger organizational patterns and dynamics operating in FSC. It became clear there were strong differences not only in the presenting questions of priority and resource allocation, but of value proposition, decision making, and communication styles. We recognized the opportunity to help them become aware of and address these patterns – to *teach them a different way to fish.*

Project Design

Holding the "Both/And" of content and process, we considered what blend of approaches would be needed to meet this client "where they were at" and enable them to create new possibilities for action.

Red Lens Perspective

We used a version of DMAIC as an entry point for design.

Define: Confirm the parameters of the work to be done

Measure: Identify what baseline data is available or needed

Analyze: Determine possible ways forward and select among them

Improve: Determine action plan for implementation

Control: Determine metrics to indicate progress

Our original thinking was to accomplish the Define, Measure, and Analyze phases in the first day, then review progress and focus on the Improve and Control phases on the second day.

Blue Lens Perspective

The CSF Navigation Process suggests beginning with creating conversations about the past and current patterns relevant to the task being addressed. The next step is to ask if those patterns are where the organization wants/needs to be in the short- and long-term.

The need for the project made it clear the answer to the second question was "no." We recognized the need to help the participants make their current patterns of interaction explicit, and to show them alternatives that would change their patterns of interaction.

Initial Project Design

With these general principles in place, we created a flow that began with pre-work and continued through the end of the second day. Here is a summary of the proposed two-day flow:

Structure for Day 1
- Opening and expectation setting
- Introduce Weighted Decision Matrix (WDM) tool
- Establish decision criteria
- Begin prioritization exercise
- Complete first pass of prioritization exercise
- Compare WDM against the criteria with strategic objections
- Clarifications & Questions – What are we going to tell the rest of FSC about what we did today?

Structure for Day 2

- Review compiled data from between-session work
- Resolve differences in perspective
- Introduce distinction between traditional strategic planning and "next smart step"
- Action Planning – Complete "Purpose to Practice" process
- What will be our indicators of success?
- What are we going to tell the rest of the organization about what we did today?
- Formal handoff to partners to reflect, make revisions, and make formal assignments
- Feedback on the day

Red Lens Perspective

We chose to introduce the "Weighted Decision Matrix" (WDM) as the tool to help focus and compartmentalize their decisions and conversations. By asking, "What criteria will you consider when making your decisions?" and, "Are each of these criteria equally important?" *before* starting into the conversations themselves, we would force the group to be explicit about these factors.

Having documented the group's quantitative inputs and listened to their rationale, each person would be tasked with re-rating the decisions based on all that transpired in the first session. This re-rating would serve as the foundation for the second day's work, where "good enough" consensus would (hopefully) be reached and action plans established.

Blue Lens Perspective

We agreed that a needed shift in pattern for the FSC leadership was to assure all voices were heard and taken into account – while acknowledging the 20+ years of history and context regarding the partners' demand to be the ultimate decision makers.

We created a process by which on Day 1 each person would independently document their inputs on Post-It notes, then have an equal amount of uninterrupted time to share their rationale before any further conversation would take place. Using the between-session time for reflection and evaluation was another deliberate change in pattern, with each participant knowing in advance they would have another opportunity to share their input in the second day.

Note: We asked participants to respond to us prior to the first session with their individual response to the question, *What should we know as consultants prior to the session to help us create maximum value for you during our time together?*

The answers were fascinating, with various participants providing feedback we were easily able to characterize in terms of our Ecosystem Dimensions. Some commented on history; others on the various Eco-subsystems (context); and others on FSC culture and stories. Some shared their motivation for joining, staying with, growing, or in one case, exiting the firm. Each one commented on the patterns of communication, power, and decision making. Each was positive about the firm and excited about the work ahead.

Project Delivery

Delivery of Day 1

All participants arrived and the meeting started on time. After covering the agenda and other housekeeping items the group moved into the first major activity, creating a Weighted Decision Matrix. Participants were on their "best behavior," following directions and honoring the time limits for their individual contributions.

In completing the exercise, participants noted that they had interpreted the categories in different ways. This resulted in the facilitators re-visiting each of the category headings to attempt to gain some greater level of consensus about their operational definitions. This turned out to be problematic – the conversation about quality ranged from the requirement to have quality as a given, to quality relative to the competition, to quality of products and services, to the quality of the client experience and takeaways.

With everyone (including the facilitators) frustrated at the lack of closure, the conversation shifted from its focus on decision making criteria to the possible decisions to be made. One conversational path focused on growing revenue from existing clients vs. acquiring new ones. Another centered on how to allocate resources among three potential lines of business. This, in turn, led to a more granular and detailed conversation about the potential for current and future marketing channels that had already been identified.

At this point, both the participants and consultants struggled to determine a clear path forward. Everyone was frustrated by the lack of consistent data and knowledge among the various people in the room. While the facilitators attempted to assure that all voices were heard, in many cases the participants recused themselves due to lack of knowledge. In an attempt to find a topic where all could participate, the group engaged in a conversation about FSC's overall strengths and weaknesses.

As the allotted time for the meeting drew to a close, participants looked to the facilitators for a concise statement of what the between-work assignments would be. Even though the consultants had mentioned early in the meeting that parts of the process would appear to be unfocused, everyone was unsettled by the drifting, sometimes chaotic nature of the flow of the second half of the meeting.

In light of the evolution of the conversation, the consultants decided that the best course of short-term action was to...do nothing. Instead, they committed to providing photographs of the work output, along with a narrative summary of the day to all participants and asked for time to reflect and discern what would be value-added activity for participants in preparation for the next session.

Red Lens Perspective

Introducing the Weighted Decision Matrix (WDM) provided the expectation of data and structure to inform decision-making. The use of time limits and facilitators also provided the expectation of structure and flow for the work. The combination of quantitative (weighting for each of the relative categories) and qualitative commentary (the ability to explain the numeric rating) provided both kinds of data to all participants.

Blue Lens Perspective

Those same tools were also important from a complexity perspective. Our intent was to change the patterns of communication and decision-making given their existing ones had not accomplished their desired objectives. In the pre-meeting communications, participants had noted that all voices were not always heard and that decision-making was based on very subjective factors. Techniques such as "going around the room" and rotating the first person to speak each time changed their traditional patterns.

Having heard that certain individuals were prone to extended monologues, providing a time limit, reinforced with a visual countdown timer, was intended to change that pattern as well. Setting the expectation that decisions should be based on pre-established criteria was yet another deliberate attempt to perturb the existing patterns of the organization.

One interesting, unanticipated conversation occurred during lunch. One of the founding partners was vigorously engaged in what appeared to be an oft-repeated debate about one particular aspect of the business. Larry observed that the conversation was not creating any new value for anyone and suggested to the partner that a different approach (more structure, visuals, showing processes from start to finish, etc.) might create a different outcome. He was very receptive and would later develop and share a 2.5-hour tutorial for those who needed it prior to the second session.

Making Sense of Day One

Denise and Larry debriefed the session the next day. We felt good about the progress made and that certain patterns appeared to shift – and less satisfied about leaving the group with a sense of frustration and lack of clear direction.

This matched well with the anecdotal feedback we received from the client. They enjoyed the structure of the first part of the morning but felt the consultants had allowed themselves to be derailed from their structure by certain members of the group. While they liked the "Post-Its," time-bound nature of the sharing, they wished for more conversation about the points where there was significant misunderstanding or disagreement.

In trying to understand what caused the confusion, we recognized how critical the lack of accurate, complete, and timely data was, and how inconsistent the levels of knowledge were about various elements of the business. This was not totally unexpected – several participants were attending an Executive Team meeting for the first time.

As an initial response, we drafted a high level summary of the meeting. We chose to de-emphasize the quantitative results due to the fact that participants had already acknowledged they had different operational definitions for the categories. Instead, we synthesized the narratives that were shared by each participant as they shared their quantitative ratings.

We also shared some higher level questions that had surfaced. These were noteworthy in that they appeared to be beyond the original scope and targets of the offsite, yet were surfaced often and with a great deal of energy and emotion.

What data is known/needed about our current way of doing business to inform future decision making (current cost to acquire/maintain clients; cost to integrate a merger/acquisition, etc.)?

Do the various leaders have the **knowledge** they need about the various aspects of the business to make informed decisions (business lines, marketing strategy, etc.)?

Is our current **governance structure** scalable? Given these conversations, does the projected future structure need to be adjusted? What roles and responsibilities need to be clarified? Revised?

Given the current context, what are reasonable **growth targets** for the overall firm? For each business?

What is a realistic planning horizon for determining **profitability and ROI**?

How do we **differentiate ourselves** from our competitors?

Note: It is important to re-emphasize that these questions emerged as the day unfolded. Viewed through the Red Lens Paradigm, we would have beaten ourselves up for not having recognized these questions before-hand. Viewed through the Blue Lens Paradigm, we were able to recognize that these kinds of discoveries emerged from the real-time interaction and could not have been known in advance.

While this discussion was taking place, unbeknownst to us one of the founding partners had an "aha" moment based on the work of the day. He was able to "cut through the clutter" of the many ideas discussed to find a "red thread" which would tie those ideas together. This culminated in a proposal document which he socialized with one of the other founding partners and selected other participants.

Design of Day 2

The positive feedback to the Partner's Proposal, along with our own reflections on the first day, created the foundation for the revised Day 2 agenda flow.

We socialized the agenda with the client's planning committee and asked them to distribute the agenda and consolidated WDM categories to the participants in advance of the next session, along with the founding partner's Proposal.

Revised Day 2 Agenda

- Opening – any other Agreements needed?

- Questions, Comments on Day 1

- Partner talks through his Proposal; with any new data/metrics in bold font. Also, any revisions based on input already received

- Affinity Exercise: What I don't clearly understand/needs further clarification; what I like most; what I am most concerned about

- Clarify and agree upon final WDM categories

- Group process for completing WDM

- Introduce Fishbone Diagram as tool to answer, "What will it take to make this happen?" Categories will be hybrid of "6M's" plus whatever evolves from earlier work

- "Sanity check" – are the areas of focus still viable? Any "show-stopper" concerns?

- Knowing what we know now, what kinds of things will each function within FSC need to focus on in the next 12 months to make this vision happen? What will be the metrics?

- How did we do in achieving the 7 objectives?

- Feedback on the day, overall process

Red Lens Perspective

The flow was designed to maximize the chance that the project's objectives would be achieved. In Day 1, we told the group the intent was to "widen the conversation" through brainstorming and exploration – even if the process felt messy and disorganized. Day 2 was focused on synthesis and focusing down to specific "Who does what by when" actions in support of the defined focus and priorities of the organization. We decided to take advantage of the Proposal already created and socialized in advance of the meeting.

Given the concern about the quantitative aspects of the WDM, we chose to repurpose it as a validation tool. For each of the (now consolidated) decision categories, our challenge to the group was, "Is there a roadblock here; a limiting factor that would necessitate scrapping the proposal or making major modifications?"

From there, we introduced another traditional quality tool, the "Cause and Effect Diagram" (also known as a "Fishbone Diagram"). Here we introduced another structured brainstorm process using Post-Its. The focus of the exercise was to identify possible tasks that would need to take place in order to implement the Proposal.

Once identified, the final task was to assign ownership of the various tasks – or at least assign someone(s) to organize and sequence the various suggestions created.

Blue Lens Perspective

We chose to build on the new patterns we offered in Day 1 that appeared to work, while incorporating our own and the client's feedback about those that worked less well.

We used an "Affinity Process" to get the group up, moving, and talking to each other to garner feedback on the partner's proposal. We created timed blocks of conversation about each of the WDM criteria to encourage more free-flowing communication.

We extended the overall length of the meeting, as well as the times for lunch and breaks to foster more informal conversations.

We continued to introduce new tools (Affinity Process and Fishbone Diagram) to showcase new potential communication and decision making tools. At the same time, we chose to retain the use of Post-It notes and making ideas visual. We stressed the objective of getting to specific action items and addressing the seven original objectives of the offsite process throughout the day to assure the participants would leave with a greater sense of closure and organization than they did after the first day.

Delivery of Day 2

The second day of the session followed the agenda to a greater degree than the first day. With no major questions or comments about Day 1, the partner "told the story" of his Proposal. He included some new data that had recently surfaced since the document was circulated to the participants. The Affinity Process used to collect high level feedback about the Proposal worked as intended.

There was some confusion as participants moved into the WDM validation exercise. This was due in part to the fact that the consolidated criteria and agenda had not been sent to the participants in advance. After several false starts, the group was able to gain clarity about the objective of the exercise (validation vs. identification of action items) and the process moved more quickly and smoothly.

The consultants requested a meeting with the founding partners at lunch. During the morning session, the partners made it clear that while they valued a sense of consensus, they were not open to traditional voting as a vehicle for strategic level decision making. This led to the question of whether there was agreement on the Proposal and if so, how best to communicate that to the other participants.

After some discussion, the decision was made for the consultants to broach the subject once the group returned to session. The positioning used was an observation – *It seems the group has agreed on the main points of the Proposal, recognizing some details may change based on gathering additional information. Did we get this right? Is there anyone with significant concerns?* There were none.

The other part of the lunch conversation was a discussion about how to address certain items that were of high interest to the participants, yet deemed to be out of scope for the defined objectives of the offsite. This was resolved by announcing to the participants after lunch the intent to drive the meeting to accomplish the stated objectives. Once that was accomplished, any remaining time would be used to talk about the "other" topics that had been surfaced. This happened in the last 30 minutes of the scheduled meeting, with some participants staying and participating for an additional 30 minutes.

Making Sense of Day 2

Immediate anecdotal comments from both the participants and consultants indicated the off site's objectives had been met, and in some cases, exceeded. From the Summary Note the consultants provided to the organization:

Our bottom line: the two-day process achieved its stated objectives – and more. Significant progress was made towards very aggressive objectives. In addition, participants learned and practiced a number of new tools to help shift their communication and decision making patterns:

- Use of limited pre-work to allow time for reflection in advance of the meeting

- "Around the room" discussion to be sure all participants have a chance to speak

- Rotating who speaks first in a group discussion

- Providing time limits for individual comments (with visual countdown timers to help all manage the limits)

- Use of Post Its to make collecting and sorting inputs easier and more visible

- Asking for and using data to inform decision making

- Use of external facilitators to drive the process and keep all on track

- Being explicit and transparent regarding meeting dynamics ("the diamond") and process to help manage participants' expectations and impatience

Notice how some of the comments focused on "traditional" measures of success, *Did you catch a fish?* while others focused on new patterns of thought and behavior. *Did you learn a different way to fish?*

The same held true for questions and concerns identified by the consultants:

The organization needs to "change the tires while the car is still moving." The daily work of the firm continues to fully engage its current resources – the action items defined will require additional time and effort.

Sequencing and integration of individual action items. It will be critical for leadership to look beyond their own individual action items to the "big picture." Who will be the "conductor of the symphony," responsible for allocating resources, managing trade-offs, and making sure the overall plan evolves as needed without being completely derailed?

The Chief Operating Officer (COO) and Director of Sales and Marketing have massive amounts of responsibility right now. For the COO: Risk/Compliance, oversight of HR and technology, managing M&A activities, developing, documenting, and streamlining processes – that is a lot to put on one person's plate.

For the Director of Sales and Marketing: Allocating marketing resources among Lines of Business and marketing channels, coordinating with Wealth Managers and the southern region; developing digital marketing, 3rd party, custodial, and direct to consumer channels – again, a lot to ask of one person.

Managing distractions/opportunities. As was stated during the meeting, potential new opportunities will surface. A process will be needed to figure out which should be rejected out of hand, which should be tabled, and which have so much potential that it is worth reallocating resources and adjusting plans to exploit them.

(Two-way) communication with the rest of the organization. Several participants noted (correctly, in our view), that the buy-in and commitment of the rest of the organization is required to make these aggressive targets a reality. *Do it because we say so* may not be the most effective way to achieve the engagement needed. It is tempting to write an e-mail or have a meeting, discuss the new direction of the firm, eat some snacks – and consider that the needed communication has taken place. We strongly urged the leadership team to consider that first communication as only that – the beginning of a process that will need to be nurtured and paid attention to over time.

Commentary - Linking the Case to the Complexity Space™ Framework

Complexity Space Framework

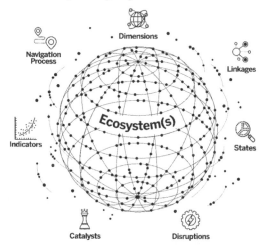

The case provides a "real world" application of the Complexity Space™ Framework. While an exhaustive evaluation would require a separate book, we will try to highlight how the use of the CSF helped raise awareness, provide the opportunity for assessment, and provided direction about how best to influence the dynamics of the FSC leadership team to provide new possibilities for different thought and action.

As a matter of convenience, we will provide our commentary in the same order that the different elements of the CSF were presented earlier in the book. Having said that, please recognize that these various elements are interconnected and surfaced at different times throughout the project.

Dimensions

History was a significant influence on FSC. Both formally, during the two days of the offsite and informally during the conversations that followed, the existence, methods, personalities, and decision-making styles of the founding partners were compared and contrasted to the leaders who joined the organization later. The founding partners were proud of their knowledge, "messy consensus" decision-making, and building their business through hustling, cold-calling grit and referrals while reinvesting all profits back into the business.

The surrounding **Context** provided additional distinctions to help explain both the current state of the organization and to point the way towards future challenges and opportunities.

While the **Political Eco-subsystem** did not appear to be particularly relevant, the **Economic Eco-subsystem** was. Much of FSC's revenue growth had been driven by a rapidly growing economy, which enabled healthy returns on invested wealth. This enabled an investment and marketing strategy that touted strong financial returns. During and after the recession of 2008, those returns no longer materialized, creating major concerns regarding how to differentiate the organization from its competitors.

The **Technology** and **Competitor Eco-subsystems** reinforced one another in their impact on FSC. The specialized market and investment analysis tools once available only to money managers became readily available to end users. Packaging those tools and making them more user-friendly spawned some new class competitors – robo-investing and financial technology (fintech) organizations.

FSC was slow to recognize these contextual changes and as a result, was forced to make significant investments in their own technology to regain relative parity in the marketplace. It was noted during the meeting that even the current technology efforts only lessened the competitive disadvantage of the firm in this area.

Changes in the **Customer Eco-subsystem** were a significant factor during the meetings. There was a recognition that the organization had been built around baby boomers, whose wealth is significant. Yet at the same time, that demographic is aging and beginning to pass on and distribute its wealth to others. The changing demographics and psychographics of younger generations, coupled with the corresponding changes in values, priorities, and purchasing preferences resulted in rich discussions about what products, services, and marketing approach would be needed for this new target audience – if it is even a target audience at all … (!)

The **Regulatory Eco-subsystem** has been a fact of life throughout FSC's existence. An uptick in governmental regulations since the 2008 recession heightened the importance of this contextual framework. Regulations due to take place within 12 months of the offsite meeting will result in some 200,000 new potential competitors as regulations would incent those brokers working on commission to shift to the same fee-based model as FSC.

The exchange about **Culture** was a rich one. Participants acknowledged that FSC has a strong culture, though they struggled to put the elements of that culture into words. Some tried to operationalize it in terms of mission, vision, and/or values statements. Others discussed it in terms of a boundary; a "line in the sand" the organization would not cross. "We would never go after clients whom we could not service with high quality." A third perspective emerged as the group referenced culture as "what everyone feels good about and commits to." Through this lens, culture was perceived as much as an end product as it was an enabling process.

The dialogue about **Motivation** shifted throughout the two days of the offsite. It ranged from the motivation of the individual participants (increase the value of their shares of stock) to positioning the founding partners to be able to (and feel good about) leaving the organization to the other stockholders, to assuring stable employment for all employees of the organization.

The operational definition of motivation expanded in other conversations to become a proxy for success measurements. Some were "motivated" to achieve revenue goals. Others to achieve a run rate that would eventually lead to revenue goals. Yet others were motivated to achieve a net profit margin in either the short or long-term.

As consultants, we helped the group to notice that the strategies to achieve each of these various possible goals and motivations were not identical. We encouraged them to hold additional discussions to help both the leadership gain greater consistency around the motivations and targets, and to help them more consistently and powerfully communicate those clear targets to the other employees of the firm.

Linkages

The concept of **Linkages** was very evident throughout the two days. They occurred at and between the many different levels we expected. There were Linkages between the two geographically separate offices. There were Linkages between the various lines of business. There were Linkages between the various wealth managers and how they approached their tasks. There were Linkages between FSC and the accountants, lawyers, and other institutions with whom they partner. There were Linkages to the various Eco-subsystems that have already been mentioned.

Our helping to name and highlight these Linkages helped to increase the awareness of the participants about two classic organizational dysfunctions: 1) *The way I do it is the only way/right way*; and 2) dismissing ideas because they were *not invented here*. In fact, we pushed the participants to leverage the opportunities in those Linkages to expand their repertoire of possible approaches to addressing their issues.

While we deliberately stayed away from providing strict content or subject guidance, we did ask them to consider whether they might strengthen the Linkages to their customers, collaborators, and other employees by conducting a series of "voice of the customer" surveys and conversations.

States

Interestingly, the CSF concept of **States** did not appear explicitly during the conversations. As we reviewed the case, the power of this element of the Complexity Space™ Framework was very apparent. Several participants commented about their comfort in their traditional, **Status Quo** models for growing and executing their retail business. At the same time, they were keenly aware that those models were not achieving the results they intended.

Their movement into a complementary line of business represented an **Innovation** strategy. It was a logical extension of their core business – in fact, it is supported administratively by centralized support staff from the corporate office.

An acquisition opportunity that emerged from FSC's foray into the complementary business line represented a movement towards **Mutation**, although probably not to the paradigm-exploding extreme we believe constitutes a true Mutation strategy.

We also found it interesting that the current State of each element of the business currently was different than where they wanted or needed it to be. The **Status Quo** needed to change – yet their experiments and innovation to change it created discomfort due to the lack of consistency and institutional processes they were accustomed to.

At different times during the offsite, a participant would raise the possibility of integrating a very different potential line of business. This was dismissed by one of the founding partners with a great deal of energy: *We are having enough trouble digesting our current lines of business – how could we possibly absorb something brand new?* By the end of the second day, he softened his stance to an openness to consider new opportunities – if not immediately, at some point during the following year.

Disruptions

The identification of the need for the offsite was the result of several **Disruptions** from both inside and outside of FSC:

- **Inside FSC:** New hires, a new organizational structure, a new acquisition, and new technology

- **Outside FSC:** A different investment marketplace, changing customer demographics and psychographics, new technology, and new competitors

It should be noted that this was not the first strategic planning exercise undertaken by the organization. Several years before, the (much smaller) leadership team had gone off-site to plot their future. While some participants did not feel that effort was successful, others noted that the internal Disruptions just mentioned were the result of intentional effort that came out of that first offsite.

Note: As will be described in more detail in the following paragraphs, we were intentional in creating our own small Disruptions within the process of the offsite. We did this in service to the client, intending to perturb their usual patterns of conversation and decision-making.

Catalysts

Like other elements of the Complexity Space™ Framework, the use of Catalysts can be viewed from several different levels. One level is the offsite itself, *What levers can we use to influence shifts in thought and behavior?* At a broader level, Catalysts focus on changes FSC can use to influence larger organizational patterns, as well as patterns outside of the organization to help them achieve their goals.

We used the Fishbone Diagram as our mechanism for eliciting the changes to be made and tasks to be accomplished in order to achieve their newly defined targets. We chose to use traditional labels for the spines of the Fishbone, believing that the participants would be more comfortable responding at that level. We chose categories that were robust enough that they could encompass the Pattern-shifting Catalysts we felt were needed.

Note: In the original seven objectives for the offsite, the focus was very explicitly on establishing the targets – determining how best to prioritize and allocate management attention and the organization's resources. The idea of establishing a plan to accomplish those was beyond the scope of our original effort. This was another case where the conversations of the group evolved, emerged, and self-organized to where it became obvious that the offsite was the time and place to at least begin that process.

The commentary that follows below is a hybrid of ideas contributed directly by the participants in post-meeting feedback and our own extension of their inputs as they relate to shifting organizational patterns.

We will evaluate the project from both our decision making process during project design and delivery and our analysis of the client's experience and project outcomes. Each section explores the distinctions and benefits of working with each of the seven Catalysts described in the CSF.

Commentary: Assessing the Experience and Outcomes from the Offsite Perspective

Catalyst: Connections
As noted in the case, we forced random seating by the participants, "around the room" input, providing time limits, and varying who spoke first to perturb their usual connection patterns.

Catalyst: Leadership
Prior to the offsite, we heard from several sources that the usual pattern of communication was highly skewed towards a few individuals within the leadership team. The use of Post-Its, making the same amount of time available for each person to speak, acknowledging and naming the unequal pattern of communication, and a specific and often-repeated request for participants to "listen hard," and to "seek first to understand before being understood" were all intentional levers used to broaden the avenues of leadership and influence among all of the participants.

Note: There were limits to how much change we could affect in this area. The senior partners remained clear, even after some gentle prodding, that their majority ownership of the company entitled them to be the final decision-makers on strategic (and any other) decisions they felt were theirs to make.

Catalyst: Stories

Requiring participants to explain ("tell the story") behind their quantitative ratings on the first day was an intentional intervention on our part to help each person provide deeper, more holistic explanations than posting a simple number would allow.

Beyond the words, it was fascinating to assess each person's conviction through the nonverbal cues and tones of voice that were used in their explanations.

At the beginning of the second day, we encouraged the founding partner to "tell the story" of his Proposal, even though he had sent the written document to the other participants in advance. Again, this was deliberate – so that the participants would see, hear, and feel the "meaning beneath the words" of the written document.

Catalyst: Risk Taking

We asked the participants to engage in several experiments through the use of the different conversational mechanisms and data collection instruments. By introducing tools and techniques that no one was familiar with in the room, we brought them all to a common level of "not knowing," which was very different for them individually and collectively relative to their usual operational process.

Note: Not all of our experiments were successful. Particularly in the last part of the first day, our intent to step back and facilitate an unstructured conversation for them to do some sense-making of the morning's inputs did not go as planned. We hoped for a broad ranging conversation. Instead, we heard concerns about the process. Where we hoped for positive expressions of movement, we heard a sense of overwhelm and lack of direction. Where we intended to leave the meeting having made fully structured assignments, we admitted a lack of clarity around future direction and left the group feeling lost.

Catalyst: Organizational Structures

For purposes of the offsite, we felt that this Catalyst offered relatively less leverage – less opportunity to influence organizational patterns within the room. The random seating, asking senior partners to be very conscious of their role, and recognizing that several participants were attending an executive team meeting for the first time are consistent with this category of tools.

Catalyst: Systems/ Processes

We spent a great deal of time thinking about the meeting process and flow before sharing it with the clients. We challenged each other to view the agenda from the clients' point of view.

While we determined approximate time frames for each piece of the agenda, we chose not to share those time intervals with our planning partners. We felt it was important to not set arbitrary limitations that could invite distracting process questions. We agreed among ourselves that we could and would be flexible based on the emerging conversations in support of that overall flow.

Commentary: Assessing the Experience and Outcomes from the FSC Participant Perspective

Catalyst: Connections

Participants suggested creating more, "high-touch" contact with their customers. The need for greater transparency and two-way communication with employees was also mentioned.

Catalyst: Leadership

The participants accepted the challenge of providing active direction and leadership to implement the actions needed to achieve their goals.

It was also understood they would need to be intentional about enabling the next level of leadership, providing them with the information, tools, and opportunities for input needed to gain their commitment and have them cascade their energy and passion to the next tiers of employees.

The opportunity to provide greater leadership to customers resulted in plans to step up credibility building activities such as publishing, presenting at professional associations and being a guest on television, radio, and social media outlets.

Catalyst: Stories

Given that the "superior return on assets" marketing model was unlikely to be viable, participants left the room recognizing a new story was needed. What will be FSC's value proposition? What will be their differentiator? The Director of Sales and Marketing was tasked with convening the various stakeholders needed to craft and disseminate this new story.

Catalyst: Risk Taking

Participants chose to invest resources in developing new(er) growth channels within their existing lines of business. They also agreed to remain open to new business opportunities – giving preference to those they could pilot fast without a significant investment in resources.

Catalyst: Organizational Structures

A major – and appropriate – concern was that if the sales and marketing strategies were successful, sufficient organizational resources were not available to handle that increased quality of business. This triggered a rich conversation about the number and type of additional resources that would be required, both to manage the clients themselves and at a leadership level to deal with the increasing complexity of the business.

Catalyst: Systems/Processes

Related to the above, a similar concern was voiced about the processes and technology required to scale. This included both the traditional process creation, documentation, streamlining, and training activities to the larger, Pattern-based question of, *What is the most flexible, robust way we can get things done to remain agile and nimble as we race into an uncertain future?*

Indicators

Throughout the two days, participants had become (sometimes painfully) aware of their lack of timely, complete, and accurate data to help them run their current business and plan for the future.

Having set goals for revenue growth, profitability, and marketing spending, participants seemed comfortable that they could measure progress towards those goals. Given their self-reported (lack of) success in following through on ambitious plans, we suggested the need for another set of metrics regarding implementation plan tracking and accomplishment.

We made the in-the-moment call to not surface the issue of Pattern-based Indicators, feeling that it would have represented an information overload to the participants at that time. We hope to surface this issue in the future.

Navigation Process

Like the previous Catalysts conversation, the process we followed to achieve our objectives can be viewed at both the project and overall business level. Since this section is being written so close in time to the offsite, we will limit our commentary to how we used the Navigation Process in designing the offsite process itself.

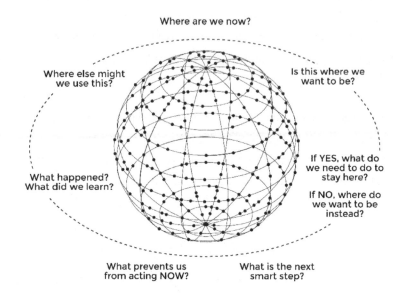

Where are we now?

Where else might
we use this?

Is this where we
want to be?

If YES, what do
we need to do to
stay here?

If NO, where do
we want to be
instead?

What happened?
What did we learn?

What prevents us
from acting NOW?

What is the next
smart step?

Where are we now? The original request for service was made by FSC looking for someone to facilitate their strategic planning offsite conversation. The original positioning of the role was as "referee" – making sure that all participants were heard and that the agenda stayed on track.

Some basic questions to the founding partner who originated the call identified that much more work was needed if the offsite was to accomplish its objectives. Being clear that ours was to be process facilitation rather than a subject matter expert role and recognizing the client was not willing to invest significant time on this process, we had to be very selective about the assessment we did at this point.

We first focused on what the desired outcome of the offsite was to be, coaching to help them understand the amount of progress that could reasonably be made in the time allotted.

We also asked for some basic information about the business itself, the history of making these kinds of interventions, and what data was available for use. The result of these inquiries was a list of the seven objectives noted earlier in the book, and a doubling of the time allotted to accomplish those outcomes.

Is where we are now where we need to be to survive and flourish in the present, near, and long-term future?

If yes, what do we need to do so we can continue to survive and flourish in the present, near, and long-term future? We learned quickly that disruptions in the internal and external environment were creating significant tension for change. It was made clear to us that ad-hoc internal attempts to accomplish the objectives had not been successful, triggering the request for external facilitation/consulting support.

If no, if we want/need to be different than we are today, what is our new desired State? While it was apparent the Status Quo was not okay, it turned out that one of the biggest objectives of the offsite was to figure out where "there" is – what the new future State could or should be.

What is the next smart step? As the participants came to grips with the idea that a more comprehensive, inclusive process was needed, it became clear that we would need to bring the clients along with us in creating the agenda. We adopted the practice of holding planning calls with a subgroup of the leadership team to provide draft meeting flows and obtain their feedback. These planning sessions would often result in follow-up questions and actions, the results of which would be folded back into the next iteration of the design.

In watching the dynamics of the client's planning team (we used a webcam application, so we had the luxury of some nonverbal input), it became obvious that there were different points of view even among this small group. As a result, we held any particular iteration of the agenda loosely, recognizing it was likely to change.

What prevents us from acting NOW? Once the agenda for each day stabilized, we made sure we had the equipment and materials needed to implement it. We divided the primary facilitation role for each agenda item between us, making those assignments based on who had the most experience in that particular tool, technique, or intervention. The other person was tasked with taking notes and monitoring the non-verbals of the participants.

What happened? What did we learn? We caucused at each break and meal to check in with each other about how things were going and what adjustments were needed. During those conversations, we adjusted time frames, focus, and roles.

Following the first day of the offsite, we conferenced with the client to get their feedback on what had gone well and what changes would make the second day more productive. As described in the case study, we incorporated much of their feedback into the second day's flow.

Where else might we use this? We tried to be intentional in continuing to "use what worked" from the first day and make needed adjustments for the second. We realized that both we and the participants were different as a result of experiencing the first day together:

- From an Ecosystems Dimensions standpoint, we now had some shared History – our work together in the first day of the offsite

- We now had shared Context and Linkages – FSC had interacted with an outside party, who brought their own technology, dynamics, and processes to the table

- During the first day we had established our own unique Culture. How serious would everyone be? How would we manage time together? To what extent would participants and consultants abide by the agreements that had been mutually defined at the beginning of the first day?

- Finally, we all had a different set of Motivations than before we met. The group shared the experience of great progress during the first part of Day One, the chaos and wandering of the last part of the day, and the question as to whether or not the objectives could be accomplished in the time remaining. This created a sense of, *we need to get focused, and stay focused on achieving those objectives. No matter what.*

"Both/And" – Again

We close this section by emphasizing again the critical importance of blending the models and tools of both the Red Lens and Blue Lens Paradigms to achieve project success. Early in the planning conversations, the client made it very clear they had little or no tolerance for theory, or other "soft and squishy" parts of the agenda.

As financial planning practitioners and business people, their primary emphasis was on setting finite goals and allocating very scarce and tangible resources in order to achieve them. Not honoring that focus would have resulted in our being perceived as not responsive to their needs.

Gaining the full benefit of the Complexity Space™ Framework depends on this ability to see through both lenses at the same time, shifting emphasis from one lens to the other as conditions dictate.

Complexity Space Framework

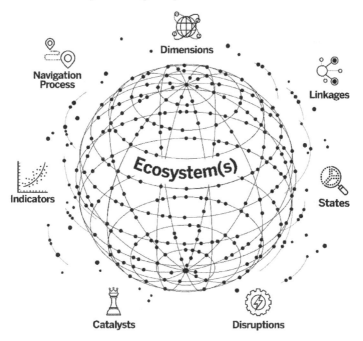

Closing Thoughts

We have covered a lot of territory in this book and thought it would be appropriate to summarize.

Our journey began in Part 1 with the recognition of a pervasive paradigm that has heavily influenced business processes and change for over 100 years – the Red Lens Paradigm. The essence of the paradigm is captured in the phrase, *We wish our organization would run like a well-oiled machine.* It assumes proportional inputs and outputs; that there is a "best way" to consistently generate desired outcomes; and that there is a clear linkage between identified causes and their effects.

We next introduced a second paradigm derived from the non-linear sciences. It focuses attention on a different set of organizational dynamics, captured in the metaphor of an *organization as an ever-changing, emerging garden.* In this Blue Lens Paradigm, the focus is on patterns of change; the self-organizing, continuously emerging, unpredictable properties of Complex Adaptive Systems. Focusing on Patterns provides a new way to identify, prioritize, and influence team and organizational thought and behavior and was the next topic we covered.

The concept of Patterns is essential to the Complexity Space™ Framework, as a specific perspective derived from integrating the Red Lens and Blue Lens Paradigms. We introduced the metaphor of viewing change through 3-D glasses – where looking through the Red Lens offers one view; looking through the Blue Lens provides a different perspective; and looking through the two lenses together provides a depth and richness of perspective not available through looking through either one alone.

In Part 2, we described each of the various elements of the Complexity Space™ Framework.

We began with a discussion of Meta patterns, patterns that span the various elements of the CSF. We next explored Ecosystem(s) and their Dimensions, deep-seated organizational patterns that are difficult to see and often even more difficult to directly influence. We discussed the importance of acknowledging the organization's History and internal and external Context, which included defining six Eco-subsystems. We also introduced the hard-to-quantify, yet extremely important dimensions of Culture and Motivation.

We continued with a discussion of Linkages. We introduced several ways to characterize Linkages and different ways that Ecosystems might connect with one another.

Any one Ecosystem, as well as sets of linked Ecosystems, can be defined by their *modus operandi*; their "State." Whether thirsting for consistency (Status Quo), targeting incremental change (Innovation), or seeking paradigm-busting change (Mutation), recognition of these States provides insight to the combinations of patterns that are likely to be at work in that particular system. What matters to an organization trying to manufacture one million identical spark plugs is very different than the organization trying to create a brand new form of transportation.

Disruptions create the tension and energy that cause systems to move within and between States. As we discussed in that section, Disruptions can take a variety of shapes, sizes, and forms. Creating a dialogue within an organization about their current State and whether or not that that will serve them in the future provides a powerful tool for strategic planning, prioritization, and allocation of energy and resources.

If Disruptions provide the energy and awareness that change is needed, then Catalysts are the Pattern-shifting levers that organizational change agents can pull to influence patterns. Seven catalysts were identified and described:

- Connections
- Leadership
- Stories
- Risk Taking
- Organizational Structures
- Systems
- Processes

We noted that each of these seven Catalysts are interdependent – changing one will, by definition, influence each of the others in some way. We also observed that there is no guarantee that patterns will be influenced in the direction that we intend. While we cannot know if a particular pattern will be changed for better or worse, we can have some confidence that it will be different.

We changed something. What, if any, difference did it make? Answering this question is the essence of the next element of the Complexity Space™ Framework and the Indicators section of the book.

We began our conversation about Indicators by acknowledging the powerful and necessary measures and metrics that are so deeply embedded in the Red Lens Paradigm. Quality, cost, timeliness, compliance, and financial metrics are all needed and legitimate ways to measure the results of an intended change.

We introduced an additional set of potential measures and metrics designed to focus attention on if and how patterns are changing. They focus attention on "weak signals" and are more forward-looking in nature. Said differently, if the traditional outcome metrics focus on, *Did I catch a fish today?* then Pattern-based Indicators provide insight regarding the question, *What did we learn about the process of fishing today?*

Part 2 continued with a description of some of the popular, prevalent, and powerful roadmaps used by Six Sigma, Lean, Agile, and ADDIE. While different in certain respects, they generally share a step-by-step approach to making change happen.

The Complexity Space™ Framework's Navigation Process is different in both its visual presentation and intent. In complex organizational systems, everything impacts and is impacted by everything else. As a result, change happens in a more chaotic, "messy" way. While Pattern-based change agents may begin with a plan, the expectation is that their plan will evolve and emerge as it is implemented. This puts a premium on rapid learning and adaptation.

In Part 3, the Financial Services Company (FSC) case provided a ground level example of the Complexity Space™ Framework in action. Beginning with the consultants' entry into the system, the case details the flow of thought and action through several cycles of the Navigation Process.

At different points throughout our presentation of the case, we introduced side-by-side comparisons to illustrate the "Both/And" integrated nature of the Complexity Space™ Framework's lenses, language, and tools.

Having described the process itself, we then revisited the case, providing a commentary linking the events of the case to the various elements of the Complexity Space™ Framework.

Which brings us to the present.

Recognizing we shared a great deal of information, we challenged ourselves to leave you with our responses to the classic journalistic challenge, *If you didn't get anything else, we really hope you got this.*

- The Complexity Space™ Framework is most powerful when it integrates the Red and Blue Lens Paradigms, not replaces them. Think 3-D glasses

- In complex systems like organizations, it is naïve to believe that change can be controlled. It is more realistic to believe it can be influenced

- New language and distinctions enable new ways of seeing, which enable new conversations, which enable new possibilities for action

- Complex, Pattern-based change requires and rewards rapid cycles of experimentation and learning. It is more productive to be curious about any given outcome than hold on too tightly with too much judgment

- The Complexity Space™ Framework is, and by definition always will be, a work in progress. This book is a statement of our thinking at this point in time, recognizing our thinking about this topic has changed literally hundreds of times over the last five years. We expect hundreds more iterations as we continue to explore it

- The best way to learn the Complexity Space™ Framework is to use it! There is no substitute for experience. Know that you can't fail; you can't "do it wrong;" you can't "break it." If we've done our job properly, the model and tools are robust – in fact, they are designed to evolve to meet the needs of practitioners trying to change patterns in their respective organizations

We hope you find value in the Complexity Space™ Framework and humbly ask you provide us with feedback. *We don't know what we don't know.* Please help us evolve this powerful tool to its next level. Contact us at:

www.complexityspace.com

dgeaston@complexityspace.com
lsolow@complexityspace.com

Denise Easton

Denise Easton is an experienced entrepreneur and consultant who works across the corporate, public, academic and non-profit domains. She focuses her research and practice on the synthesis of complexity science, change management, knowledge management and strategic organization development. She is the Managing Partner of Complexity Space Consulting and Founder and CEO of Adapt Knowledge.

Ms. Easton graduated from The College of William and Mary. It was through her certification as a "Human Systems Dynamics Professional" (HSDP) by the HSD Institute that she first collaborated with Larry Solow.

Ms. Easton has published in numerous publications, peer reviewed journals and co-authored a course for the Plexus Institute titled" The Complexity Lens". She recently authored Chapter 22 *"At the Crossroads of Organization Development and Knowledge Management"* for the book, *"Organization Development in Practice"* edited by William J. Rothwell, Jacqueline M. Stavros, Roland L. Sullivan, and John Vogelsang.

Lawrence Solow

Working at the intersection of people, processes, and strategy, Lawrence (Larry) Solow helps clients discover new possibilities for action. Larry has 30 years of internal and external change management experience working in a variety of market segments in both the profit and not-for-profit sectors.

He earned a graduate degree in Organizational Communication from Temple University following his BA degree in Human Communication from Rutgers University.

Mr. Solow is a Six Sigma Black Belt and has been certified as a "Human Systems Dynamics Professional" (HSDP) by the HSD Institute. Larry has presented at ASTD, SIETAR, IQPC, IAF, SHRM, Project World, Project Summit, Chaos Network, and other major professional conferences.

Mr. Solow co-authored, *"What Works for GE May Not Work for You: Using Human Systems Dynamics to Build a Culture of Process Improvement."* He also authored Chapter 9, *"A Comprehensive Approach to Organizational Learning: Total Learning Architecture"* for the book, *"Learning Architectures: Building Organizational and Individual Learning"* by Warren R. Wilhelm.

Early Praise for Complexity Works!

"In *Complexity Works!* Larry Solow and Denise Easton update our tools for understanding and productively transforming today's organizations. This book explains practical insights to help shape cohesive strategies and improve execution. *Complexity Works!*...by helping us more holistically identify what's really going on...and our choices...so we can 'see it big, yet keep it simple'."

Julian D. Kaufmann, Chief Human Resources Officer,
G100 Companies

"*Complexity Works! Influencing Patterns in Teams and Organizations* bridges what we know about change and what we need to learn about complexity to influence Pattern-based change. Leveraging a Red Lens and Blue Lens view of complexity gives leaders and organizational change professionals a new framework and practical ways to approach change work."

Christi Olson, PhD, Head of Organization Effectiveness and Employee Development, Stanford Linear Accelerator Center, National Accelerator Laboratory

"By combining the Red Lens and Blue Lens you will understand organizational change in a dramatic new way, and manage it about ten times better. Your mind will open."

Dr. Warren Wilhelm, President, Global Consulting Alliance; and former Chief Learning Officer, Amoco and AlliedSignal

Made in the USA
Coppell, TX
22 November 2020